BORN IN 1964?
WHAT ELSE HAPPENED?

RON WILLIAMS

AUSTRALIAN SOCIAL HISTORY

BOOK 26 IN A SERIES OF 35
FROM 1939 to 1973

War Babies Years (1939 to 1945): 7 Titles
Baby Boom Years (1946 to 1960): 15 Titles
Post Boom Years (1961 to 1973): 13Titles

BOOM, BOOM BABY, BOOM

BORN IN 1964? WHAT ELSE HAPPENED?

PUBLISHED BY BOOM BOOKS

Wickham NSW Australia
Web: www.boombooks.biz
Email: jen@boombooks.biz

Creator: Williams, Ron, 1934- author
Title: Born in 1964 : what else happened? / Ron Williams.
ISBN: 9780648651147

Cover image: National Archives of Australia.
A1200, L48570, "Everyday Australian";
A1200, L49401, Australian steelworker at BHP;
A12100, L46545, Sheep farmers;
A1200, L49486, High School social.

TABLE OF CONTENTS

IMPORTANT PEOPLE AND EVENTS

Queen Elizabeth II	Queen of England
LI Robert Menzies	PM of Oz
Arthur Calwell	Opposition Leader
Pope Paul IV	The Pope
Lyndon Johnston	US President
Alec Douglas-Home	PM of Britain

WINNERS OF THE ASHES

1961	Australia 2 - 1
1962-3	Australia 1 – 1
1964	Australia 1 - 0

MELBOURNE CUP WINNERS

1963	Gatum Gatum
1964	Polo Prince
1965	Light Fingers

ACADEMY AWARDS 1963

Best Actor	Sydney Poitier
Best Actress	Patricia Neal
Best Movie	Tom Jones

SYDNEY TO HOBART YACHT RACE

1963	Astor
1964	Astor

PREFACE TO THIS SERIES

This book is the 26th in **a series** of books that I have researched and written. It tells a story about a number of important or newsworthy Australia-centric events that happened in 1964. The **series** covers each of the years from 1939 to 1973, for a total of 35 books.

I developed my interest in writing these books a few years ago at a time when my children entered their teens. My own teens started in 1947, and I tried to remember what had happened to me then. I thought of the big events first, like Saturday afternoon at the pictures, and cricket in the back yard, and the wonderful fun of going to Maitland on the train for school each day. Then I recalled some of the not-so-good things. I was an altar boy, and that meant three or four Masses a week. I might have thought I loved God at that stage, but I really hated his Masses. And the schoolboy bullies, like Greg Favel and the hapless Freddie Bevin. Yet, to compensate for these, there was always the beautiful, black headed, blue-sailor-suited June Brown, who I was allowed to worship from a distance.

I also thought about my parents. Most of the major events that I lived through came to mind readily. But after that, I realised that I really knew very little about these parents of mine. They had been born about the start of the Twentieth Century, and they died in 1970 and 1980. For their last 20 years, I was old enough to speak with a bit of sense. I could have talked to them a lot about their lives. I could have found out about the times they lived in. But I did not. I know almost nothing about them really. Their courtship? Working in the pits? The Lock-out in the Depression?

Losing their second child? Being dusted as a miner? The shootings at Rothbury? My uncles killed in the War? There were hundreds, thousands of questions that I would now like to ask them. But, alas, I can't. It's too late.

Thus, prompted by my guilt, I resolved to write these books. They describe happenings that affected people, real people. In **1964,** there is some coverage of international affairs, but a lot more on social events within Australia. This book, and the whole series is, to coin a modern phrase, designed to push the reader's buttons, to make you remember and wonder at things forgotten. The books might just let nostalgia see the light of day, so that oldies and youngies will talk about the past and re-discover a heritage otherwise forgotten. Hopefully, they will spark discussions between generations, and foster the asking and the answering of questions that should not remain unanswered.

The sources of my material. I was born in 1934, so that I can remember well a great deal of what went on around me from 1939 onwards. But of course, the bulk of this book's material came from research. That meant that I spent many hours in front of a computer reading electronic versions of newspapers, magazines, Hansard, Ministers' Press releases and the like. My task was to sift out, **day-by-day**, those stories and events that would be of interest to the most readers. Then I supplemented these with materials from books, broadcasts, memoirs, biographies, government reports and statistics. And I talked to old-timers, one-on-one, and in organised groups, and to Baby Boomers about their recollections. People with stories to tell came out of the woodwork, and talked no end about the tragic, and funny, and commonplace events that have shaped their lives.

The presentation of each book. For each year covered, the end result is a collection of short Chapters on many of the topics that concerned ordinary people in that year. I think I have covered most of the major issues that people then were interested in. On the other hand, in some cases I have dwelt a little on minor frivolous matters, perhaps to the detriment of more sober considerations. Still, in the long run, this makes the book more readable, and hopefully it will convey adequately the spirit of the times.

Each of the books is mainly Sydney based, but I have been **deliberately national in outlook**, so that readers elsewhere will feel comfortable that I am talking about matters that affected them personally. After all, housing shortages and strikes and juvenile delinquency involved **all** Australians, and other issues, such as problems overseas, had no State component in them. Overall, I expect I can make you wonder, remember, rage and giggle equally, no matter whence you hail.

WHAT HAPPENED IN 1963?

There was no doubt about what the two top stories were in 1963. **Firstly, there was the murder of Gilbert Bogle and Margaret Chandler.** The bodies of these two people were found on New Year's morning on the banks of the Lane Cove River that flows through a well-to-do region of Sydney. Both of these had CSIRO affiliations, and had left a party together, and had not been seen since. Their near-naked bodies were found, and this caused a sensation in the news-starved papers of this lethargic January period.

No matter what theory the police came up with, and there were dozens of them, none of them stood up as more information was revealed. It was agreed that some sort of poisoning was involved, but not much else was agreed upon. By the end of the year, no one was charged, no one apparently was even a suspect.   Fifty years later it was suggested that the simple truth was that they were not poisoned by anyone, but had laid down on the river bank and had breathed in marsh gas that is formed by decaying matter in swamps. And that caused them to die. Having said that, there are still many facets of the story that are not explained by that theory, and it is hard to see the theory surviving.

The second big event of 1963, was the killing of John Kennedy. The media have worked this over so thoroughly and so many times that I need to add little. All I can say is that Australia was as deeply shocked as the Americans, and that here the feeling of loss was very great. The strong relationship we had with America was unaffected, and our friendship with President Lyndon Johnston remained as the cornerstone of our commitment to US foreign policy. Though not everyone was happy with that all the time,

SOME THOUGHTS ABOUT 1964

In closing my 1963 book, I mentioned a few **international matters** that I thought would become more important in this 1964 year. They are worth recounting again in brief now, so we can keep an eye on them as we proceed.

The first of these was political situation in Indo China. There, the nations of Laos, Cambodia and Vietnam had been granted independence by France a decade ago, and over that period, had managed enough economic success to show they could stand on their own two feet, but the Communists had gradually been becoming more powerful. Of course, Communism was a dirty word in America, and the US was committed to removing it from the face of the world. Given that we generally supported most of America's foreign policy, it followed that if the growth of the Reds there was troubling the US, it was also worrying us. So, if the worst came to the worst, it might be that we would be taking up arms again sometime in the near future. Certainly, the diplomatic stances taken by the Yanks and the Chinese at the moment suggested that this would be the case.

The second matter related to various forms of atomic bombs. Here, we were fortunate enough to have a variety of choices, that ranged through the plain-vanilla type that was dropped on Japan, up to the top-of-the range model of the cobalt bomb. By now however, we were all pretty tired of being scared by the prospect, and by the US-USSR (China) posturing, and so much of the endless propaganda peddled to us fell on deaf ears. Still, every now and then, we all thought about it, and shook our heads about how the hell we got to this position.

The third was the violence flaring in many parts of the world as coloured people fought for freedom or for a better deal. For example, in the US, and South Africa, and Africa, the black races were fighting against massive imbalances in wealth, income, and power between themselves and the whites. So far, our own Aborigines had shown little tendency to emulate this violence, and neither had the New Guinea natives. This, however, was something to watch.

DOMESTIC POLITICS

Robert Menzies was our Prime Minister. He was head of the Liberal Party, and was very comfortable, completely unchallenged within his Party, and with a fair majority in both Houses. The zeal that he had suffered from in his early years had almost gone, so he was down to sober management of the economy, and keeping one jump ahead of the Opposition. This he was doing very well.

The Labour Party Opposition was led by Arthur Calwell. He had been a Member of Parliament for two hundred years and, according to my father, had one of the most astute Labour minds of the 1850's. He was a true, old-fashioned Labour supporter, and had never become reconciled to the fact that this nation thought that the practice of socialism had gone out with cement horse troughs. He was struggling with a divided Party, and the chances of Labour winning any future election seemed to be zero while he remained leader.

The political scene was fairly benign. The major problem was that Australia was certain to lose its markets in Britain as the Brits moved into the Common Market with European countries. Our current deals with the Brits were not all that profitable, but they were secure, and there was not much marketing involved. It looked as though in future, our sales reps would need to go out to the world and sell, sell, sell. This transformation was not all that welcome for many.

Then there was Communism. Communism at the time in Australia had two faces. The first, the international one, was constantly forced into our gaze by our American friends, who spent much of their energy trying to prove that their Capitalist system was superior in every way to the Communism of Russia and China. We in Australia were awash with the propaganda that this effort generated, and part of Menzies' bag of tricks was to frighten us constantly with the potential terrors of the Red scourge.

The other face of Communism in Australia that was visible was in our Trade Unions. Many, in fact most, of our Unions were controlled by Communists. This was not, in general, because the workers were in favour of international Communism, but rather because the local Reds were well organised, and prepared to go out on a limb against the perceived vices of the local bosses. These activists thought that the strike weapon was the right one to use, and so the nation was always plagued by tons of impromptu strikes. Menzies was annoyed by these strikes, but that did not stop him from exploiting them. He could condemn them to the full as damaging our national economy, and at the same time he could point out that this was part of the Red strategy to conquer the world by internal subversion.

OFF WE GO

So now you are ready to go straight into 1964. I hope you survive it really well. First, though, I will provide some information on how I structured this book

MY RULES IN WRITING

Now we are just about ready to go. First, though, I give you a few Rules I follow as I write. They will help you understand where I am coming from.

NOTE. Throughout this book, I rely a lot on reproducing Letters from the newspapers. Whenever I do this, I put the text in a different font, and indent it a little, and make the font somewhat smaller. **I do not edit the text at all.** That is, I do not correct spelling or grammar, and if the text gets at all garbled, I do not correct it. It's just as it was seen in the Papers.

SECOND NOTE. The material for this book, when it comes from newspapers, is reported as it was seen at the time. If the benefit of hindsight over the years changes things, then I **might** record that in my **Comments**. The info reported thus reflects matters **as they were seen in 1964**.

THIRD NOTE. Let me also apologise in advance to anyone I might offend. In a work such as this, it is certain some people will think I got some things wrong. I am sure that I did, but please remember, all of this is **only my opinion**. And really, **my opinion does not matter one little bit in the scheme of things. I hope you will say** "silly old bugger", **and shrug your shoulders, and read on.**

So now we are ready to plunge into 1964. Let's go, and I trust you will have a pleasant trip.

JANUARY NEWS ITEMS

General de Gaulle announced that he was prepared to play ball with other nations **after France got the H-bomb**.... He already had the **ordinary atom bomb**, but he went on to say that he was determined that **France would become a leading world power**. Only then was he prepared to co-operate with other European nations so that an entente with America could become a reality.

The Queen's New Years Honours list was published. Top honours went to **knighthood**s, and dozens of distinguished Australians gained these. There were also honours of a lesser kind that went to former **Oz Test cricketers** Alan Davidson, and Neil Harvey....

A knighthood was also received by **Sir Frank Worrell, former West Indies cricketer**. He joins the select group of knighted ex-players that is made up of Don Bradman, Jock Hobbs, Pelham Warner, and Len Hutton.

The Victorian Government will approach the Federal Government and ask it to finance **an entymologist to study bush flies for three years**. They have reached plague proportions in the State, and are a non-stop nuisance in Western Australia and Tasmania. The Premier said that **no one knows anything much about flies**, and a nation-wide campaign was needed to eradicate them.

A fisherman and his three mates netting off the coast at Kempsey, NSW, landed **240 jewfish in a single haul. Each fish weighed 30 to 85 pounds**. This was considered a record haul for the area. **Wise words from Bob**

Menzies. "I tell my colleagues that if I win elections, all will be forgiven. If I lose, I will catch the earliest and slowest ship to the furthest corner of the earth".

A prestigious group of US scientists yesterday announced that they had researched and found that **there is a strong link between smoking and cancer.** This was the first major study world-wide to say this. They called for action to adjust behaviours to counter this effect. **They said that pipe smokers were not affected.**

A Victorian car-driver **drank about 50 glasses of beer** before he killed a girl on a road crossing. He started drinking at 5.30am, and stopped at 6pm. He did not stop after the collision, and said when apprehended "you did not expect me to stop, did you? **I haven't got a licence, and the plates are off my brother's car."**

The Federal Government announced that it will soon start giving **grants to public and private schools** for the creation of **science facilities in High Schools.** The Government was very shy about giving money directly to private schools because of some **considerable opposition to it.** But this was a clever way **to achieve much the same result.**

A Letter-writer to the SMH decried **the growing practice of keeping hens in batteries.** In making his point, he felt the practice was so new that he had to explain it to the reader.

A Dr Linge, from **Canberra,** pointed out that there were **only two public lavatories** in that fair city.

THOSE HAZY LAZY DAYS OF SUMMER

Australia, as was usual at this time of the year, was on holidays. The schools had four more weeks of holidays to go, most workers had another fortnight, and families had swapped either to the coast, or to the country, to get away from it all. And they did that, especially this year. There was scarcely anything to worry about. **Within the nation**, jobs were plentiful, food and housing and clothing were affordable, and money could be borrowed. Most people had access to a car, the Hills Hoist was still twirling in the breeze, the Victa often started, and the Sunday barbie was never to be missed. In all, in general, it was a nice place to be.

Looked at from the nation's point of view, things were pretty good. Prime Minister Menzies, in his address to the nation, dashed off this cheery message.

"The task of every Australian in the New Year we are entering will be to continue to build on the strong foundations established not by our generation alone, but by the great-hearted people who pioneered our country and their descendants.

"I feel sure that in 1964, and after, we can look forward to prosperous development. We, both Government and people, must not be satisfied with what we have or what we have done.

"There are challenges to be met and together we can produce a driving force which will give Australia an enhanced place in the world and a better life for her citizens,"

In other words, "Things are going pretty well. I know you are not going to listen to any serious problems at the moment, so I won't give you my normal message of moderate gloom and parsimony".

Internationally, there were only a couple of hot spots that you could worry about right now. **There was Cyprus.** In that island, the Greeks and Turks had been at each other's throats, since WWII, over which of these two nations should have the upper hand in Cyprus. It looked (to the naïve) as though this had been settled in 1959 by the UN intervention that more or less said that Cyprus should be independent of both. Now, however, this agreement was unfolding, and tempers were flaring, and swords were rattling.

Then there was North Borneo. This was under the suzerainity of the new nation of Malaysia, but the Indonesians were saying it should belong to them. There were clashes on the borders, and infiltration of "terrorists" into Borneo, and handfuls of fighters from both sides were being killed every few days. Still, the Brits and Malaysia both said that the situation was under control, and that Australia troops would not be needed to sort out the Indonesians, so this was no immediate cause for worry.

That was just as well, because Australia was ambivalent about what to do if we were asked to intervene. **On the one hand**, we were still strongly tied to the British Empire, and so wanted to help if any part of it was threatened. **On the other hand**, why would we antagonise Indonesia, our nearest neighbor, by getting into a fight with them? At the moment, we were very good friends with them. Why would we jeopardise that friendship? Let's hope we don't have to make that decision.

Certainly, in the early weeks of this year, no such decision was at all necessary, and so the wonderful weeks of summer idling could continue without qualms.

Gradually, though, the world got back to its natural agro condition, and some real news filtered through. The first of this was a tragic incident in the outback.

DEATHS NEAR BIRDSVILLE

News item: A family of five English migrants has perished on the edge of Sturt's Stony Desert, about 60 miles from Birdsville. They apparently had car trouble, and started to walk, but appeared to have become lost and walked only a short distance from their car. The temperature in the area reached 110 degrees in the last few days. They had found a well, but the water was too heavy to carry, and at the end they could not find their way back to the well.

The Sydney Morning Herald (SMH) produced an Editorial on this, and back came this response.

Letters, A Brain. Your editorial comment on the Birdsville Track tragedy remarks somewhat complacently that it is unlikely to be the last. We should make sure that it is the last. I suggest the following obvious measures:

(1) That permission be sought from police or other competent authority, to cross such a dangerous area. That permission only be given when the authority is satisfied as to mechanical reliability and sufficiency of water, food and fuel.

(2) That time of anticipated arrival at destination be given.

(3) That the track be clearly marked with stone cairns, oil drums or any other unmistakably clear object.

(4) That at intervals of say 10 or 15 miles there be deposited tanks containing water and that these be replenished regularly.

Comment. These are worthy ideals, but not practical in this land of scarce resources.

A BRAND NEW IDEA ABOUT SMOKING

For a couple of years, there had been some talk about trying to establish a link between smoking tobacco products and lung cancer. The tobacco industry in Britain threw up its hands in horror at the thought, and late last year officially ridiculed the idea.

Now, however, a large study over a number of years found smoking was a definite cause of cancer, and that the more you smoked, the greater the chance of being affected. This challenged perceptions in all quarters. Most Aussies were completely surprised. The smokers in particular went straight into denial. The tobacco industry took the obvious approach of saying that the research was faulty, that it was a fluke result, and that they had multiple results suggesting that no one should take any notice of it.

The world health industry was concerned. Some part of it was already convinced. That was why the study had been started in the first place. For the most part, it simply took the cautious approach and said that more evidence was needed. The complicating factor was that many in the health industry were smokers themselves, and it was hard for them to accept that, if the study was right, the sensible thing for them was to give up smoking.

In Australia, most people put the controversy onto the back-burner. "I know a man who smoked five ounces of tobacco a day for a hundred years, and he lived to be 200". "Look at Winston Churchill. He smokes cigars all the time, and he is still going strong." At this stage, it was a sensible attitude when confronted with a **single** research result, because it was true that there **were** examples everywhere of smokers living to a ripe old age (of seventy). Slowly, ever so slowly after this, the message got through, and the number of smokers now has shrunk to less than 20 per cent of the population.

The Federal Government was suddenly caught with a serious health issue that it had no concept of. If the study truly represented the situation, what could the Minister do? Lamely, and not at all understanding the consequences of the study, he told the nation that restricting advertising would do the trick. Then he went on to say that there were all sorts of reasons why he could not do this.

The issue was wider than that. Over the next few weeks there was a deluge of Letters that probed everything that was known about smoking at the time. I provide a diverse sample below.

Letters, Mrs Barbara Bennet. I don't get it. I am not allowed to read "Lady Chatterley's Lover" or "Tropic of Cancer." I cannot readily buy and use opium and or hashish. I must have a chest X-ray. My car must be guaranteed roadworthy before it is registered. All for my own good---to save myself from myself, so to speak.

Yet I and, more importantly, my more impressionable younger fellow-Australians are constantly bombarded by advertising media which glorify the smoking of cigarettes into something so romantic, thrilling and satisfying that not to indulge in this desirable, status-giving habit is equivalent to announcing that finer things of living, leave us cold.

Now that we hear from America of the proven dangers of cigarette smoking, isn't it time for my protective Government to save me from myself again by taking away the temptation of the proffered packet? Or am I being incredibly naïve?

Letters, H Levien. It is nonsense for the Commonwealth Minister for Health to say that the Commonwealth has no power to control advertising from the tobacco industry. It could, if it had the interests of the community at heart, prohibit cigarette advertising over television and radio stations through its control over licenses to operate these stations.

The most important purpose in suspending this advertising would be to reduce the influence on teenagers who have not yet taken up smoking or who have only recently acquired the habit.

Letters, Mrs M Alderdice, Kirribilli. Last year, as a result of a car crash, I suffered serious injuries, one of which was the complete collapse of one of my lungs. Oxygen was of course administered, but on recovering consciousness several days later I found to my dismay that added to my difficulties was the fact that other patients in the ward were smoking (and playing transistor radios incidentally) and that despite my complaints nothing could be done about the smoke.

After my discharge from this hospital, I suffered further serious complications to my lung and had to be readmitted to another hospital because of this. This time I was in a two-bed ward, but found to my amazement that at one stage the other patient was a very heavy smoker (also with a transistor radio) as were most of her visitors. When I complained to the sister in charge I was told that I was too old-fashioned. So I pointed out to her that even on public transport provisions were made for both smoking and non-smoking compartments, of which one had a choice, but apparently, of all places, one didn't have a choice in a hospital.

For a long while after my discharge from hospital I was extremely sensitive to polluted air of all kinds, particularly smoke caused by cigarettes, but this I could not escape while in contact with the public. I'm beginning to feel, however reluctantly, that in order to protect oneself from this menace we may have to resort to some sort of mask, as did the people after World War I in the great flu epidemic.

Letters, Mrs H Van Monsjou. Why should the cigarette companies suffer any more than the breweries? If they are going to tell people it is harmful to smoke, at the same time tell them it is harmful to drink alcohol in excess.

Letters, W A Perrett. Norman Jones' letter chides the Minister for Health, Mr Sheahan, for his reluctance to legislate to control or prohibit smoking, but the fact is that any such legislation would be impracticable.

However, there are ways in which smoking could be discouraged by legislation and it is surprising that Mr Sheahan has not thought of them. Also, an existing piece of legislation could be enforced by the government.

I refer to the prohibition on the sale of smoking materials to juveniles. Shopkeepers break the law thousands of times every day, and I have yet to hear of a prosecution although Government inspectors quickly pounce on anyone who sells certain harmless and necessary commodities at the "wrong" time. Then too, the rash of cigarette-vending machines gives juvenile smokers an incredibly easy source of supply.

In view of his compulsion complex with chest X-rays, fluoridation, hair sprays, etc., it's a wonder Mr Sheahan, as guardian of NSW Health, hasn't thought of making cigarettes harder to get by confining their sale to tobacconists and hotels, and allowing vending machines only in places inaccessible to juveniles.

Letters, A Sinclair. Why all the fuss about taxidrivers being banned from smoking on duty? What harm does it do to the passengers, or what effect has it on the prestige of the service?

The Motor Transport Department says that a driver should be able to refrain from smoking while he has a fare, on a trip which may take any time to finish. He may just finish a trip, then almost at once pick up another fare. I think this is really unfair; if smoking is such an offence, it is about time the authorities set about the filthy habit of people smoking at the table in eating-houses.

Letters, Thomas M Thick, Kingsgrove. Having been under treatment by ear, nose and throat specialist, I booked a seat in a first-class non-smoking carriage on the "Spirit of Progress" on October 4 last year. I had the mistaken but snobbish idea that first-class passengers were more certain to observe the non-smoking regulations of the Railway Department.

When the Spirit steamed out of Sydney station, out came pipes and cigarettes, creating a Sydney bus-like atmosphere. No effort was made by railway officials to enforce the regulations, and only a few refrained from smoking when appealed to.

The same conditions prevailed on Victorian country trains. I returned to Sydney from Melbourne on the "Daylight" on October 16, when non-smoking regulations were strictly observed---a pleasant trip.

Comment one. It would be unfair of me to criticize the slow reactions of the Feds to the release of this research. In a twinkling, it changed attitudes, and economic consequences, of the nation that had stood for as long as anyone could remember. Smoking then had so much glamour attached to it, and now the smoker is forced outside of most establishments. Mind you, that has taken 50 years, and maybe still has further to go.

Comment two. Smoking then, and now, played an important part in the Australian budget. The Government gets a huge amount of excise from it. For those close to the budgetary process, this has always been a matter for consideration.

Comment three. Notice that there are no comments on the study itself. They are all about how smoking affects the writer. No one had any knowledge about the etiology of smoking, nor of the probabilities involved, nor of the health processes. These came only with research, gradually, over the years.

A GOOD MONTH FOR GROUCHES

Every January, as the reporters and editors of the newspapers immerse themselves in the oceans round Australia, the volume of bad news slows down, and that provides an opportunity for correspondents to grizzle. Not that they don't do it in other months, after all "writing a Letter to the Herald" is part of the therapy for being upset. At this time however, there is more available space, and the chance of being published goes from minuscule to minute.

These grizzles also suit me fine. They give me a chance to run quickly through various aspects of Oz society as it was at the time, and acquaint you with some of the things that people were talking about. Good background stuff.

Below, I present a few pages of the best grizzles this season.

Letters, Robert Young, Sydney. One rarely associates originality of thought with a municipal body but the ingenuity shown by the Waverley Council in imposing **a double entrance charge** to the Bondi Beach dressing sheds, once for undressing and again for dressing, reaches a new low.

That the immoral and probably illegal innovation has aroused public resentment is evidenced by the decreasing patronage to this once crowded convenience, and the cash receipts must be less than when the previous procedure, of giving patrons taking their shorts and shirts to the beach a re-entry ticket, prevailed.

Letters, Mrs N Bialoguskil. As a normally easy-going Aussie I must admit I am surprised myself at how strongly I feel about our local well-established SP betting shop in the main shopping centre, close to the hotel for the convenience of customers coming and going, and in the next street to the police station.

I feel it is a sad undermining of basic principles when a society, supposedly based on law, openly and flagrantly and continuously breaks one of those laws with the seeming condonation of our police officers, who are sworn to uphold and protect them.

Non-enforcement of gambling laws undermines respect for the structure of law as a whole when authorities let one section of society so blatantly abuse it.

Comment. SP betting and gambling were everywhere. Every pub had its bookie, sometimes two. Two-up games and baccarat games flourished at night, and floated round to avoid the occasional police raid. Of course the cops knew where these offenders were, and of course they earned a packet by ignoring them. Maybe, it is hoped, they will all go away if the new law opening TABs is passed.

Letters, Bridget Gilling. I am cranky. I am offended by vulgar and ungrammatical television commercials, cigarette advertisements, puerile and tasteless comics, women's magazines extolling weddings rather than marriage and implying spinsterhood is failure, high pressure door-to-door salesmen, poker machines---the list is endless, certainly long enough to occupy censorship-minded people and allowing them to leave literature, temporarily at least, in peace.

Letters, A Collis, Burwood. Is it not time some action was taken to prevent anti-social behavior of smokers? On at least five occasions during the past fortnight I have travelled in clearly designated non-smoking railway compartments in the company of smokers, who, I assume, could not read or chose to ignore the notices. The journeys were not made at peak hours, and there was more than adequate accommodation for them to sit in the compartments provided for smokers.

Letters, Tom Burke, Cowra. The recent report of injuries caused by bottles left on a Sydney beach illustrates a growing menace that is State-wide.

In the country we find camping reserves, roads, riverbanks and waterholes littered with discarded bottles, most of which are eventually smashed by sportsmen with rifles or driven over by motor vehicles.

The use of cans is a slight improvement---they will rust away in time---but a bottle lasts for years, menacing the community with cut feet, damaged motor tyres, and the dread of all rural dwellers, the bushfire.

Letters, E Boote, North Sydney. In the "Herald" last week we read of picnics on the lawn at the Oberon Prison Farm. We also read of the Minister of Justice, Mr Mannix's enthusiasm for "rehabilitation."

Violent crime has greatly increased since "rehabilitation" theories have been put into practice so much in recent years. Drastic punishment is a deterrent, picnics aren't. In fact, a potential criminal could be encouraged to commit crime by the cynical thought that he would be rewarded by "rehabilitation" for doing so. It would not be so bad if prison farms housed minor offenders only. Such, however, is far from being the case.

Apparently we members of the public are expected to tolerate criminal attacks on our children just to gratify the State Government's desire to be liberal to criminals (though not to the potential victims of criminals.)

THE TAB IS COMING, PERHAPS

The NSW Government is being very brave. It appears that it will go ahead and establish off-course totalisators throughout the State. These will allow punters to place bets legally on race meetings, and do away with the illegal SP bookies. The latter group have much money riding on opposing this new system, and despite current mumblings, might yet stop the introduction of the TABS.

FEBRUARY NEWS ITEMS

Another great tragedy. The month started with the news that eight toddlers had been **burned to death as they slept in their cots in a day-care nursery….**

This occurred at Templestowe, a suburb of Melbourne, at about 4pm, **when the children were having their afternoon nap.** Two others were saved. **Police do not know what started the blaze, but it was not bushfires.** The three-roomed nursery, built of timber and asbestos cement, was destroyed in 20 minutes.

Despite **our uncomfortable relationship with Communist China,** figures released show that China is now **our biggest customer for wheat.** We send six per cent of our exports to China, and import only half of one per cent of our imports from there.

The American House Committee on Immigration has asked the US Government **to cancel the visa of actor Richard Burton** because of **"immoral behavior.** It is a matter of public morals", said the Chairman….

The Congressman went on to say that Burton and Elizabeth Taylor have openly been carrying on their affair, even though Taylor is still married to another man. He did not mention that Taylor is expecting her divorce to come through within days….

Defiant Liz said: **"Wherever Richard goes, I go."**

Britain and France have announced that they **will build a 21-mile (rail only) tunnel under the English Channel.**

British actor Peter Sellers is to marry 21-year-old Swedish actress, Britt Ecklund. He has known her only for a few weeks, "and she truly is one of the most beautiful girls I have ever met". She accepted his long-distance phone proposal.

News item. February 13th. **Richie Benaud yesterday played his last game of cricket for Australia.** He retired at the end of the Fifth Test against South Africa, a series that was drawn.

Arthur Upfield died at the age of 71 last night. He was famous in Australia for **creating the Aborigine sleuth, Detective Napoleon Bonaparte, and writing over 30 books about him**. He hit the big time in 1931 when "The Widows of Broome" sold 210,000 hard-back copies in America alone.

The NSW State Government will in future **give four weeks annual leave to all of its 160,0000 employees.** It is expected that the other States will follow suit soon. Times must be prosperous. The unions are happy, **now**.

Ballet dancers **Dame Margot Fonteyne and Rudolf Nureyev** will perform in **Sydney and Melbourne in April**. This will be in conjunction with the Australian Ballet Company and orchestra. This will be her third tour of Australia. Nureyev was here for a private visit in 1962.

New item, February 28th. The **NSW Legislative Assembly passed legislation approving off-course betting shops**. This will go to the Upper House on Tuesday, and might then become law. It might not, too.

HMAS VOYAGER SUNK

News item, February 11th. The Australia destroyer Voyager sank off Jervis Bay, NSW, after mid-night last night, after colliding with the Australian aircraft carrier Melbourne.

The Melbourne is the flagship of the Australian fleet, and was carrying 1,000 men. The Voyager was carrying 300. It was cut in two, after a head-on collision. It was reported a day later that three persons has been killed, and 239 were missing. No personnel from the Melbourne were affected, though the vessel itself was badly holed. It was proceeding at a slow pace to Sydney.

News item, February 13th. Three men and 79 missing are the official toll of the sinking, though the Navy is of the opinion that all 82 will be lost. Beaches along the coast, and coastal waters are being thoroughly searched for survivors, though there is now little hope of finding anyone.

Questions are being asked how such an event could occur in fair weather, and with all the radar and other technology available. The Prime Minister has decided on a public enquiry, in the form of a Royal Commission, and that will remove it from the province of the Navy.

The Feds announced that compensation will be paid quickly to the family of the dead, and compensation will be provided for those injured. The payments appear at first glance to be reasonable, and in fact paid quickly. But, I will get ahead of myself a little by saying that compensation for **injuries with a delayed impact** has remained controversial, and even fifty years later, some of them have not been settled.

News item, February 20th. The British Government offered the use of a vessel, similar to the Voyager, to the Australian Navy, on loan for an indefinite period. That makes it a gift. The Oz Cabinet is inclined to accept it.

HAVE STAMPS BEEN STAMPED OUT?

Letters, Collector. With the GPO in the public eye at present, due to the recent exhibition, it seems opportune to draw attention to a practice which is not creditable but which appears to be growing.

This is the removal of stamps presumably by some postmen or postal officials before delivery of letters. This is particularly apparent about Christmas time when so many letters and greeting cards arrive from overseas. The foreign stamps, naturally, appear to have particular attraction.

My personal experience includes letters from Belgium, Argentina, Malaysia, etc, while at present I hold an envelope from Canada from which the stamp has been carefully removed. No doubt other folk could confirm this by similar experiences.

This little Letter made me stop and think. What has happened to my stamp collection? I had one as a lad, and spent many a night with my tweezers and hinges and catalogues happily taking stamps off envelopes, and sticking them in albums. My magnifying glass was always at hand, as I perused every single stamp looking for the mistake in the printing, or the colouration, or the perforation, that would make me a fortune.

As it turned out, fortunes passed me by but, slowly adjusting to this, I remembered that in 1964, a large part of the population collected stamps from all their letters, and some of them were serious enough about collecting that they were worthy of the title "philatelist". Where have these all gone to? What happened to philately?

I asked an old-timer from Armidale these questions. He has collected stamps all his life, and has a big network of friends all over the world who send each other stamps. He agreed that the amateur has died away. He put it down **firstly** to the huge proliferation in the number of stamps issued. Every country, about 1950, woke up to the idea of commemorative stamps. These were special issues to celebrate anything at all, and these were sold to supplement the normal day-to-day stamps. This raised good money from collectors, over and above their normal postage needs. So, as the 200 nations of the world each pumped out commemorative issues, more and more, the trickle gradually turned into a glut, and the scarcity value fell to zero. Amateurs stopped collecting.

Secondly, my old-timer also said that in 1950 it was uncommon but possible to find flaws in stamps, and that these were the pot of gold that many people sought. Since then, the techniques of production had improved enormously, so the number of faults was ever so much smaller. No gold, no diggers.

Finally, he added, that so much mail is now posted with an imprint, rather than a stamp. There is no fun in collecting imprints, he said. "You might as well collect empty bottles".

Let me close this rambling with a reminder of some other fads and hobbies that have disappeared. In the war years, I can remember collecting the cardboard tops out of free milk bottles delivered to schools. Then, the cards from Nestles penny chocolates. Later, there were cards from petrol stations, and they made long drives more fun. Later still, and even to this day, there were various types of football cards.

I wonder, and do not know, what kids collect now. Maybe it is all done on a computer. I hope not. In any case, how long has it been since you had a game of marbles? Or jacks, for that matter?

THE GOOD OIL

I know you have been waiting for some up-to-date news on goannas, and I am happy that some has now arrived.

Letters, Kelvin Green. The letter from Mrs. E. M. Taylor surprises me as I have been bitten a few times by goannas in the course of years in the bush, but I have never had any recurrent breakout from the wounds like she describes. In fact, the reptiles didn't make any wound.

Believing the tales of the old bushwhackers, I used to kill the difficult goannas each time I saw them. Curiosity however, caused me to examine their stomach contents each time, and I found the goanna's chief foods to be large grasshoppers, a few frogs, and a lot of large spiders, venomous ones among them. This sort of finding finally discouraged me from killing any more goannas!

Although I have never experienced the bite of the "Water Dragon," as a certain goanna is known, I am quite willing to accept the word of naturalists that he has powerful jaws and can do damage. His food is chiefly fish caught in Australian rivers. The harmless stumpy-tail is to believed by some people to be a relation of the Mexican Gila monster. Other than being a lizard, he is no relation and is no more dangerous than a pet tortoise. In fact, many people like to have one or two of them in the gardens as an inoffensive bit of wildlife. I can recommend the extension of this practice.

In the Western Australian wheat belt I became acquainted with a large, bronze-green goanna with a yellow tail. I found him protected by a solid body of opinion of farmers. This reptile goes down into the burrows of rabbits, and eats the rabbit kittens, a habit which, needless to say, does the country no harm.

WOOL IS STILL OUR MAIN EXPORT

There was plenty of money in wool, and plenty of problems. One big problem was that synthetics of various types had been round since the war, and they were eating more and more into the Oz overseas market for wool. The Australian Wool Board had set up a marketing group that was selling the virtues of wool, and Sir William Gunn was the prominent spokesman for that group.

In the last decade, different types of synthetics had come to the market, and for a time had been able to claim superior performance. For example, in the 1950's, I wanted never to press shirts, so I bought a wardrobe of Bisley nylo-poplin 666 shirts. They worked very well for a while. No ironing, easily drip-dried. After about six washings, though, they started to yellow, and the material became thin, and looked permanently crumpled. Even I had to admit they were not suitable for wear, and brought out the iron again.

Some had better experiences than I did, and many of them had worse. So, the jury was still out on synthetics. These two Letters below put some of the arguments for wool.

Letters, A Turner. I can assure Mr Scott that there is no fabric blended of man-made fibre and wool that will not crease in the humid conditions of our summer climate. Note, too, that blended suitings, although light in weight, are not as cool as pure wool. There are all-wool suitings weighing only 9oz per yard that will not crease under any conditions, but it is a matter of price. A man will pay £1,500 for a car, but ask him £40 for a summer suit and he will tell you he is being robbed. Retailers who are always playing down the price of men's suits, and who are always seeking to take a little bit more out of them, have only themselves to blame. Man has yet to make a fibre having all the attributes of wool.

Letters, A O'Brien. Mr E Scott criticises the quality of lightweight materials for men's suits. Had he purchased 100 per cent wool he would have no grounds for complaint. As woolgrowers we wear only 100 per cent wool and have found even the most badly creased suit or frock is free from creases after 12 hours on a hanger. I was astounded a few days ago to see one of our leading department stores (with whom the majority of woolgrowers in this State would have accounts) advertising wool synthetic suits for schoolboys. Having clothed my son in pure wool, and speaking to mothers who have used the blend, it is obvious which material is really "boy-proof."

What use is there in Sir William Gunn being given more money to promote wool when our own manufacturers and retailers are so busy promoting blends which, as Mr Scott says, are rubbish"?

Comment. Wool has kept its position in the market. There is no place for it in the world of t-shirts and jeans, but wherever reasonably classy clothes are worn, wool is prominent. Even in high fashion clothes, very fine wool is in strong demand. So too it is in colder climates.

SOME CHANGES IN WOMEN'S CLOTHING

After the war, women's fashions went a bit wild. As more material became available, and as different and more colourful fabrics hit the market, women gradually cast off their wartime austerity, and sometimes became very jazzy. I can remember about 1950 that my eldest sister, then in her courting years, turned up in what was called a French skirt, and completely wowed us. It really was just a very flamboyant skirt, with an extraordinary mass of material, puffed out in all directions, and if you saw it now you would laugh out loud at it. Then, it was seen as a break with the austerity, and the drabness, and the slacks, and the second-hand clothing of the war years, and was the epitome of what the young spunk should be defiantly wearing.

The emancipation of fashion continued on, and in 1964, things were pretty chic. Yet, there were some customs of the past that lingered on. For example, lots of women still wore corsets. Very few would leave the house without stockings and garters or suspenders. The Letters below throw some more light on women's fashions at the moment.

Letters, Norma Shiels. Once again fashion decrees that women's slacks and shorts, which till recent years were solely a man's attire, are so designed that they must be zippered at the sides or, more ridiculously still, zippered at the back. I often wonder just why women are forced by our fashion experts, the ones who should be taking the lead in design, to wear such garments.

Apart from the fact that openings at the side and at the back of slacks and shorts are extremely awkward to undo, the resulting design does the very thing we women try so hard to avoid, that is they accentuate the tummy. There is nothing that does this more than a tight waistband and a perfectly flat front on slacks or shorts.

Having recently returned from a world tour, I was agreeably pleased to see many women and girls in overseas countries wearing slacks and shorts having front openings; some plain, others nicely decorated with frills or pleats, fancy buckles and wide belts, and others nicely ornamented with several buttons down the front. What an improvement on the flat fronted things that we have to wear in this country. It is all right for us to have front opening skirts and dresses, so why not our shorts and slacks?

Letters, Barbara Bennett. Your writers can jest about and criticise the current shift style of dress, but I am willing to stick my neck out and affirm that we women owe a debt of gratitude to the designer of the ubiquitous shift only equaled by the debt we owe the designer of the brassiere in its modern form.

I have seen shifts being worn by women of all shapes and sizes and aged from 8 to 80 and, do you know, as long as they fit as they should, snugly round the hips, I am sure they look better on most figures than many, many of your modern garments, for example, stretch pants.

For the expectant mum in the early months of her pregnancy they are ideal: similarly for the post-natal period before her figure returns to normal. What bliss to be able to shop, corsetless, secure in the knowledge that the odd tummy bulge is camouflaged.

I have seen smart linen shifts that do not look out of place at a race meeting. Lined Thai silk shirts are heaven for after-five wear and believe me, "Modeste", they not only look comfortable, they are, and who doesn't look her best when she is comfortable and relaxed.

NEWS AND TRIVIA

Letters, J Groutsch. Presumably the purpose of the Army's decision to allow Papuans, New Guineans, Asians and persons of mixed blood to serve in the previously "all-white" Papua and New Guinea Volunteer Rifles is to increase the membership of this entity. If this is so, it is hard to believe that this purpose will be achieved.

The only new recruits who will be entitled to the same gross pay as their white brothers-in-arms (34/ a day, including the expatriate allowance) will be a handful of Asians and mixed bloods who have the right of entry for permanent residence in Australia. The rest will have to be satisfied with the princely pay of 4/11 a day.

Despite the Army's grandiose gesture, the Papua and New Guinea Volunteer Rifles still remains an exclusive club.

Letters, Peter McKenzie. Recent reports of surf rescues have continued to perpetuate the erroneous concept that one of the hazards of surfing is the "collapse" of sandbanks.

Sandbanks are particularly solid features which, although they can be gradually moved or eroded, are neither hollow nor sufficiently topographically accentuated to be considered "collapsible"! The most common cause of surfers' sudden difficulties, and almost always that the cases attributed to "sandbank collapse," is a rapid change in rip current conditions.

These currents, which drain seawards through the surf zone, are controlled by a variety of factors, two of the most important of which are the waves and the tide. As the tide falls, the currents become more concentrated in their channels, which may become insufficient for the quantity of seaward draining water, particularly after a sequence of larger than normal waves.

Under these conditions the rip currents may suffer rapid changes in direction or increase in number by development of subsidiary currents across sandbanks with sometimes alarming results for the unwary surfer. The banks do not, however, "collapse."

TRIVIA: WINE IS NO LONGER PLONK

Liquor reforms in all states were starting to be felt in 1963, and the alcohol scene was slowly becoming more civilised. One of the reforms was the removal of the old wine bar from the back entrances of pubs, and the elevation of wine to a beverage that was something more than a pony of port, musket, or sherry in a dirty glass.

Table wines were making inroads from Europe, and the consumption of wine at home with meals was becoming fashionable. Mind you, the Aussie table wines were sometimes not so good, but Penfolds, Queen Adelaide, Coonawara, and Cawarra were names that were gaining a good reputation that lasted. Many people were coming to grips with the new brands from overseas and were still thinking in terms of clarets, rieslings, moselles, burgundies, without getting more specific.

But, our wine industry was on the verge of a big growth period, and at the start of the period of development that would bring it near the top of the world in quality.

MARCH NEWS ITEMS

The **battle of the tuckshops was on.** Hordes of barbarians, in the guise of well-meaning mothers, were taking over school tuckshops, and **banning meat pies, sausage rolls, and cream buns**. In their stead, they were proposing ghastly stuff that children hated, like **the dreaded Oslo lunch**. Likewise sweets and soft drinks were on the outer….

One writer suggested that, to protect teeth, **instruction in the use of toothpicks** should be given, so that children could clean their teeth this way. Perhaps they could have exams on the subject. **Grrrr….**

March 11th. **The Queen gave birth to her fourth child, a boy, tonight.** He has not as yet been named.

March 16th. **Jack Ruby was found guilty of the murder of Lee Harvey Oswald**, the killer of President John Kennedy. The jury took only two hours to reach their verdict, which was that he was sane at the time of the shooting. **A death penalty will be ordered**, but it cannot be carried out for at least two years. The verdict will be appealed.

The trading hours of shops in all States are carefully regulated. Union rules are preventing State governments from allowing shops to open longer or at more convenient hours….

In NSW, shopkeepers have lobbied for years and have had no satisfaction form the Government. Now a trader, fined one Pound for late trading, has **said he will go to prison rather than pay the fine….**

The Independent Traders Association has recommended that **all others similarly convicted should also refuse to pay**. **The State Government is worried** that there will be a number of traders sent to gaol, and this will damage it status with the voters.

A horticulturist at the University of Wisconsin claims that **thunderstorms make onions sick**.

Malaysia and Indonesia are still menacing each other. The Malaysians have introduced National Service for the purpose of training their young men in war-like pursuits. Now, the Indonesians have, in response, called on volunteers to register to "crush Malaysia".

The Health Department of the Northern Territory has told an Aboriginal couple living in residential Darwin that **they must get rid of their 13-year-old pet boar**. An inspector to their house found that it was spotlessly clean, the pig was neater than any dog in its habits, that it was perfectly safe because it had no teeth, kids play with him and ride him like a pony, and he stands on his back-feet and begs like a dog. **It is a pet,** he found. Still, **neighbours have complained and he has to go**.

One of Australia's **most favoured sons has been killed in a car crash**. **It was Frank Partridge, a winner of the VC for conspicuous bravery**. Apart from that, he became famous for winning many quizzes on **Bob Dyer's Pick-a-Box TV show** in 1961. He won about 12,000 Pounds in prizes.

The Easter holiday is here, and **10 people died on NSW roads in the first day**. This is four more than last year.

OPPOSITION TO THE BEATLES

An octogenarian, Mr Howard Ashton, got the month off to a good start. He had been observing the Beatles for some months, and had been dismayed at the way in which people of all ages were reacting positively to them. For example, in a Letter to the *SMH*, he stated that the British Prime Minister and Leader of the Opposition had both instructed candidates for upcoming elections to make sure they included references to the Beatles in their speeches. "Could a more disgraceful scramble for the votes of fools be imagined?"

Ashton turned his wrath to the young fans of the Beatles. "The young morons who scream and faint as part of the ritual … is only another example of the depths of teenage stupidity in the least fortunate of their generation of the dull, the idle, the failures; those whose sloppy speech, untidy dress, and beatnik beards and bad manners are doing such harm to the youth of today."

He had some criticism too for the negroid pop songs, the recording of moronic screams, and the hoots of the Beatles. He pointed out that there was already a Beatle market in sham music and records in Australia, and "some of the feeblest teenage groups are preparing their yeah, yeah, yeahs for the coming visit of these high priests of vulgarity."

Up till this point, Mr Ashton's entertaining Letter would have had grunts of approval from lots of parents and older folk. Then he went on to blot his copy-book with many of these. He compared modern youth to the "Roman low-grade teen-agers of the Augustan age" and cast doubts on whether **the degeneracy he saw now** would allow us to **withstand future overseas aggressors** if we were attacked. There was quite a jump in time in his argument, almost 20 centuries, and an equally impressive jump in his logic. Still, his Letter attracted a number of responses. Let me point out before I give the detail of these that there were a couple of respondents who simply said that he had hit the nail on the head, and they agreed fully with him. Others were more inclined to argue.

Letters, Mrs Mavis Robertson. I should like to think that when I am 80 I shall turn my anger to better use than Howard Ashton.

Mr Ashton is angry with the youngsters who follow the Beatles. He suggests that the true heroes are the warriors, from ancient Rome to the Anzacs. Beatlemania is certainly not heroic, but then neither is war. This is the age of the Bomb as well as the Beatles. Neither the Bomb nor the Beatles were the creations of teenagers.

I am angry with society which knows that young people need heroes and yet can offer them no more than the Beatles. I am angry with all the adults who cash in on the desire of young people for bright, lively entertainment by promoting cults for profit. I am angry with any adult who then blames the teenagers for the inadequacies of our society. But most of all I'm angry with anyone who tries to tell young people that war is a possible path to greatness.

Letters, Mrs E Allworth. As a "sober," but not uninformed, mother of a hardworking third-year honours student, on a Commonwealth scholarship at Sydney University, I am sorry to contradict such a highly respected judge of good taste as Mr Howard Ashton

My daughter and I both delight in the excellent theatre, music and art to be found these days in Sydney for the looking, but although we don't scream, we both love the Beatles, they are such good fun.

Could Mr Ashton be a little out of touch?

Letters, J Fossey, Balgowlah. In his attack on Beatlemania, Howard Ashton seems to have become angry for causes that are lost and for standards that are no more.

He seeks to glorify war and the warrior spirit. I doubt if war was glorious in the days of the Emperor Augustus; I doubt if it has ever been really glorious; and I am positive that World War II and the horrible little Korean War were anything but glorious in our own time.

The Beatles are a passing fad. They may amuse us or dismay us, or even disgust us, but they seem to be far preferable to the philosophy of the Caesars, of Napoleon, or of Hitler who "purified" thought, eradicating "vulgarity" and "decadence."

Do not let us be angry about four young men with long hair who sing in a fashion, causing a few girls to swoon. Let us breathe deeply of the air of freedom and liberalism, which allows vulgarity and nonsense to live side by side with refinement and culture and learning.

Letters, Mrs Jill Stephan. In reference to Howard Ashton's letter on the need for anger against the Beatle cult, I wish to make several points, I am not an expert in teenage psychology although I do have a teenage daughter stricken to some extent with Beatlemania. Strangely enough, examination results tend to show that she is not a moron.

I respect Mr Ashton's views, and at one time I would have felt inclined to agree with him. But I now see that this division of young people into two camps, one of which swoons over inadequate idols and the other which possesses creative intelligence and a saner adjustment to adult standards, is a false one.

There is indeed a division. One that exists among all age-groups and which is marked as it has always been by intelligence and character. If some Beatle-lovers appear uncouth and ill prepared for life it is for reasons that go far deeper that passing infatuation for singing idols. There is always a "low-grade minority."

Because our own youth was made more sober by war, this does not mean that our children are not capable of becoming adjusted, overnight if necessary, to a more serious and demanding world. I, for one, am not afraid for the new brood of Anzacs. It is clear that, under our present social system and for reasons that I shall leave to the experts to work out, our teenagers are determined to become enraptured with some cult or another.

Personally, I prefer the charm of the Beatles to that of many of the young American entertainers. Far too much protesting is done by adults about this harmless group of likable English boys.

Letters, Mrs J Brown. How I pity Howard Ashton! It must indeed be galling to have to sit back and watch teenagers enjoying themselves. I am the mother of a 17-year-old son and I buy him Beatle records as I was a depression teenager and missed out on the normal fun that kids of that age should have.

As for young people of the "sober families" that Mr Ashton mentions, they will not necessarily prove themselves in war. From what I remember of the last war, it was the "larrikin" who first volunteered for service, often paying the supreme sacrifice, while the so-called educated ones jumped hastily into protected jobs.

The thing that worries me is that these irresponsible "Beatle maniacs" will have to lay down their young lives protecting grumpy old people like Mr Ashton.

Letters, Joan Jones. Howard Ashton's letter has stimulated me to express a long-felt revulsion at the mass imbecility in most unexpected places---not only the teenage bourgeoisie, but their parents and grandparents even, who laugh at and encourage such "beetlebrainery." Is it quaint and appealing to disport oneself the way the "modern" teenagers do? I find it eccentric and revolting.

If a responsible citizen shuffled along the street in weird clothes, his hair to all appearances undone, and muttering "Yeah, Yeah!" one minute and screaming inanities the next, would he be allowed his freedom? Of course not, but one need only be under 20 years, say, and most people would smile indulgently with the attitude: "Well, you're only young once."

I lament that Mr Ashton's remarks will not strike home to those it should most concern---those in authority over us. It seems to be their attitude that no law is worth considering if it loses them public favour, loses them votes or unsettles their own enjoyment of their elevated positions.

STRIKE A LIGHT YOU STRIKE A LOT

If I wanted to, I could easily write a book on the biggest, best, or silliest strike for the year. No matter what else in happened in the Oz community, strikes were always there, and could be relied upon to disrupt the lives of millions of different people many times every year. In a world that was changing so rapidly, it was nice to have something reliable that you could cling to.

This little episode below is a good example. I don't need to explain it, because you will pick it up easily. It is a good example of a strike that came for no real reason, and then went, without a trace. Just one of the many thrills of life.

Letters, Sailor's Wife. I would like to ask all those busmen who went on strike on Wednesday, was it so urgent? Relatives, friends, mothers, and children of the men of HMAS Voyager had to make their own way to Garden Island.

Letters, Indignant. Isn't this just another of the selfishness of the employees of our transport system to strike at the moment of national disaster when hundreds of anxious relatives are unable to visit official offices in their desperate search for news of their loved ones? Surely it should be the patriotic duty for these employees to suppress their selfish impulses until the situation is clarified.

As usual the public suffers from the inconsiderateness of the Australian worker.

Letters, F Wilson. Of all days that should have been a day of mourning for all those brave men who are missing and lost in the sad Voyager tragedy, the bus men had to choose Wednesday to distress and upset the public, many of whom would be mourning the loss of their loved ones.

Bus men should hang their heads in shame.

Letters, A Read. The Transport Workers' Union apparently considered that many Sydneysiders were incapable of choosing their own penance for Lent, hence they imposed one of their own choice, and as a result old ladies, expectant mothers and others had to walk to church on Ash Wednesday.

Letters, L Nicholson, Albert Road, P and C, Strathfield. On Tuesday, February 4, members of the Australian Tramway and Motor Omnibus Employees' Association staged an unauthorised lightning strike, at Strathfield, leaving a school full of mentally retarded children, all functioning on less than half the mental capacity of a normal child, stranded on a boiling hot afternoon, without bus transport.

These men were fully aware of the nature of the pupils using the bus from Albert Road School, yet no warning was given, and no provision made for these children. The principal learned by accident of the situation, but not all of the parents could be contacted.

Administrative staff and a transport inspector from Burwood depot were as helpful as they could have been, but could do very little of a practical nature to help, as the depot was taken over by malcontents responsible for the unscheduled strike.

Many children had to be marched to the station in the heat, early enough to catch their usual train, thus disrupting their work schedule for the afternoon; some had to walk a long distance home, and some were driven home by the principal of the school, who was still at his desk at 5.45pm.

TA-B OR NOT TA-B?

Every time you think that the NSW has to make a decision at last on the TAB, it squirms out and leaves the question in the air. On the surface it seems simple enough. Should you take a long-standing system full of people- and police-corruption in disgraceful premises, run by seedy underworld figures, and replace it with an honest transparent system in good premises run by small businessmen? Should the massive profits of gambling go to the SP bookies and their molls, or should they be shared among the taxpayers? Should bets be placed in the back lanes of pubs illegally, or should they be placed in proper business premises in the full light of the law?

The answer seems obvious, and indeed it should have been. But the vested interests and the bribes paid to many people in positions of influence tended to confuse the thinking processes.

While the argy-bargy was still going on, the proponents of one side or the other kept up their barrage of arguments for their particular side.

Letters, Rev Richard Campbell. The debate in the Legislative Assembly last Thursday about locating TAB agencies away from schools, churches and hotels is fascinating.

What intrigues me is the automatic inclusion of churches in this list. Do our parliamentarians think that the Church, cast into the role of the moral conscience of the community, cannot face the realities of community life?

If so, this is disturbing, for how is the Church to show the relevance of its basic gospel of redemption if it is surrounded by an air of unreality? Are the scruples of churchmen thought to be so delicate that their pious sensibilities will be shocked by the sight of people acting as they now legally will? Or is there here an inadequate understanding of God, in that a church building is somehow thought to be His special domain, far removed from the corrupting influences of society?

On such a theology, if indeed betting shops are the invention of the devil, perhaps they should be next door to the church where the Almighty can keep an eye on them.

Letters, Piggott, NSW Temperance Alliance, Sydney. It is to be hoped that objectors to the dumping of a gambling centre near their church will not be misled by any clause prohibiting same.

The Liquor Act very clearly gives a ground of objection (Sec 29F) "That the premises are in the immediate vicinity of a place of public worship, hospital or public school."

Over a great number of years I have on various occasions appeared as an objector to a licence on this and other grounds. But what the Bench considers "near" is a totally different conception from that of the ordinary individual. I could cite many cases, but I remember one case where the distance was only 13 feet. The whole thing is a sham, delusion and a snare, and it will prove so with TAB.

STOP PRESS

At last a final decision has been made **on the TAB. Yes, it will go ahead.** A board will be set up, with 9 members, two from the State Government and seven from racing interests. These latter will not include any SP bookies. A General Manager will be appointed. No policy decisions will be made until all members have been appointed and discussions have been held.

NEWS ITEMS AND TRIVIA

Library Services. The first municipal library service was reported in 1954. Since then about half the nation's Councils had set up services. Some of them were full on, with branches in several convenient places, and others barely managed a single outlet. Others said they had none because of lack of money, and some said because of staffing.

The Letters below give a glimpse of what the situation was at the time.

Letters, Irene Young. When we moved to Hornsby Shire from the town of Forbes 13 years ago, we were assured that a shire library would be established "shortly."

How is it that a small town like Forbes can be culturally so far ahead of the Hornsby Shire? Let country folk who have had a good town and shire library but also the benefit of borrowing from the Sydney Public Library consider themselves fortunate compared with their poor suburban relatives!

Letters, John Payton, Orange. Kathleen Jensen points out the difficulties involved in establishing a Blue Mountains library service as its area covered a distance of 17 miles from Katoomba, 22 townships and 500 square miles.

She should come to Orange where four adjoining shires were glad to collaborate with the Orange City Library to form a regional library with two bookmobiles to service the area. Their runs are up to 50 miles from base. I don't know how many townships but every little school in the area and about 25,000 square miles of shires and towns are served. They make available to 42,000 people, a library of 40,000 books so there is a good choice. Any book asked for will come on the next trip of the bookmobile in perhaps a week, certainly within two weeks.

The borrowers pay nothing. The whole lot costs the shires under £10,000 a year and the city the same.

Subtract from that about £6,000 Government subsidy and everybody is happy. And, and this is the nicest thing about it, every child at school outside of Orange is called on and invited to read a book which was made to interest him. Children who read books are on the beginning of the road to becoming educated and intelligent citizens.

Comment. It should be remembered that many towns and suburbs still had libraries left over from the Schools of Arts that had been popular in many towns between the two World Wars. These institutions were now going into terminal decline, but they offered bodies of books that had in the past served people who had no other access to books at all. To that extent, they served a useful purpose while the municipal libraries found their feet.

MENACE OF FAT COMMUNISTS

Letters, H Parkster, Valley Heights. Your editorial states that Prime Minister Sir Alec Douglas-Home has put the view that Britain believes a fat and comfortable Communist is likely to be less of a menace than a lean and hungry Communist.

When an African alligator has completed the swallowing of his tenth District Officer, he does not become less dangerous. Rather he looks avidly about for the eleventh, I notice that the principal occupation of millionaires is acquiring more millions. Fat and well-fed pirates have been dangerous in the past, and there is no reason to suspect that a fat and well-fed Communist will be any less realistic about the aims of a lifetime in the Marxist cause than a lean and hungry one.

Those people who wish to trade with the Communist world ought to back their activities by stating their real object, which is the acquisition of wealth. Recourse to this type of nonsense makes their arguments highly suspect.

Comment. I was brought up in the Cessnock coalfields in NSW, and there was a lot of Reds in the pits. As I look back, I can remember say 20 Reds quite clearly, and not one of them was fat. I wonder now whether there is a lesson there for me. Does it mean that these scrawny men were all the more dangerous because they were lean and hungry?

I am inclined to think that they were. When, at age 18, I went to Sydney University, the Commos there were tame, fat, glossy imitations of the ones from home. All they talked about was getting traffic lights across Parramatta Road outside the Uni. My home-grown agitators had pit-top meetings that urged workers to take control away from management, and mixed it in with a great measure of class hatred, and angry talk about the coming revolution, and the daily suggestion that we "empty our water bottles and go home".

Maybe Douglas-Home **was** right

A LION TRAGEDY

Four circus lions escaped from their cage in fields six miles from the centre of Adelaide. On the way out, they tore their trainer to pieces and ate parts of him. The trainer had looked after them from birth. They roamed in the field for two hours, after which the trainer's body was discovered, and their absence was recognised....

Police were called and they, and a couple of sharp-shooters, managed to shoot three of the lions. The fourth one went back into the cage without bidding.

APRIL NEWS ITEM

Total **attendance at Sydney Easter Show** this year reached the total of **1,082, 822**. Quite a mob.

The UN was in adventurous mode. It wanted to see if **ships manned by a mixture of nationalities** would work. So it assembled a crew from Britain, West Germany, Italy, America, Holland, Greece, and Turkey, and put them on board the US Biddle. **The trial will last a year….**

No alcohol is permitted aboard US ships, so there will not be a daily tot of rum for the Brits. Prayer mats will be provided….

After a year, the trial was of course labelled a success. However, it was **decided not to use it in future**.

A University lecturer, Dr Maurice Benn, in Perth **was sentenced to death for the murder of his 4-year-old son by shooting in the temple with a .22 rifle….**

Counsel said that the boy made animal noises, ate with his hands, and had little or no recognition of his parents, ran round with his tongue sticking out, could not talk. He had no recognition of right from wrong. **Benn's wife had been worn down to the verge of collapse….**

Ben gave evidence that he had a fear of **what the boy would go through in life**, and was afraid his wife would have a breakdown. **The death penalty is still carried out in Western Australia**, but legal circles expect that the State Executive Council will commute the sentence.

April 6th. General Douglas MacArthur died yesterday.

Mr and Mrs Cohen, **shopkeepers** of Newport Sydney, have been taken to gaol for week **for refusing to pay a fine for the late closing of their shop....**

If any person pays their fines, they will be released **even if they want to stay. More shop keepers are lining up** to get a stint in gaol....

Next day. Mrs Cohen was released when her fine was paid by a third person. She did not spend a night in gaol, but said she hated it.

Be warned. The Beatles will be coming to Sydney soon. On April 12th, three schoolgirls started a queue, at 7am, for tickets for their first performance **on June 18th.** The ticket office will open at 10am. But not on April 12th. **Tomorrow.** By 8pm last night, there were 60 people in the queue.

The young **Deputy Leader of the Labour Party, Gough Whitlam**, in outspoken comments, considered the reasons **why his Party had lost the last elections.** One reason he said was the fact that his leader, Arthur Calwell, did not perform as well as Menzies. He also expresses dissatisfaction with the Party organisation and the manner of selecting candidates. **These were fighting words....**

These were rare public utterances within the Labour Party. If he continued along these lines, clearly he was destined either to be a quick and complete failure or, possibly a bright success. **Maybe we will hear of him in the future.**

DOES BILLY GRAHAM STILL WORK?

In 1959, the American evangelist Billie Graham, and his very big retinue, visited Sydney, Melbourne and Brisbane, and while there, preached sermons to masses of people at venues like the Sydney Showground. His idea was to start a Christian revival, and to encourage people to offer their lives to his God.

The tour was a great success, with hundreds of thousands attending about 10 performances, and thousands of volunteers ready at all times to harvest those who made "decisions for God". Most of the Protestant churches gave the crusade their blessing, and the Catholic Church refrained, though it placed no obstacles on its members attending.

The question that was often raised at the time was the one raised by Mr Smith below.

> **Letters, David Smith, Moorebank.** It is now five years since the American evangelist Dr Billy Graham was in Australia for his most remarkable crusade in our capital cities. At that time, Dr Graham said that it would be four or five years before the real, lasting effect of the crusade could be realised.
>
> At this stage, it would be of interest to many of your readers, no doubt, to hear if any of those who made decisions at Dr Graham's invitation are still standing by the decision they made and, if so, what real change has been evident in their lives. It would also be interesting to know what lasting effect is currently evident in Churches as a result of the crusade.
>
> On receipt of this Letter recently, the SMH commissioned a Staff Correspondent to work out the lasting effects of the campaign.

He reported that there was some anecdotal evidence that the benefits were still being felt. He gleaned this by interviewing the clergymen of the leading denominations, and asking about any changes they had noticed in their flocks. They said that there was a small increase in its size, and perhaps in the Sunday-plate of donations. One said that the number of youths joining the clergy had increased, and that the ability of the churches to work together had been increased.

The Methodist spokesman in Victoria, however, was negative, and said that "the results are not commensurate with the enormous amount of money, time and endeavour and organisation spent in the crusade."

In considering the above, you would expect that these clergymen put the best possible light on the episode, and that other opinions were possible. Fortunately for us, the material presented above spurred a number of writers into comment.

Letters, LS, Victoria. Whether we can assess them or not, there must be lasting good effects from Billy Graham's Crusade. My reason is that I feel definitely that despite his methods and some of his beliefs, the Spirit of God was in him and active through him.

Letters, Rosalie Paix. Regarding the permanent results of Dr Graham's crusade, it is very obvious that those Churches who prayerfully and expectantly put all they could behind the crusade were the ones who reaped lasting and immeasurable benefits. Two aspects not mentioned in your article were the thousands of Bible Groups still existing as a result of the crusade and the many who still gather for and prayer for Dr Graham and the leaders of our Governments, a powerful force, indeed.

Letters, Rev E Marks. Some excellent people who made decisions for Christ during the crusade attend our church. Their lives are an inspiration to us all. The failure of those who fell away should not necessarily be attributed to Dr Graham or the crusade as such. In some cases it is an indictment on the local church or minister for failing to follow up the person concerned.

It is pertinent to remember that, even among those who made decisions to follow Our Lord during His ministry, not all stood with Him until the end. Further, in the regular week-by-week work of the individual evangelical church, it is a fact that some who register a spiritual decision fall away. In this respect, the Billy Graham crusades simply follow the pattern of normal church life.

Comment. These first three Letters were more or less what you would expect. They are quite supportive of the aims of the Crusade, and ready to call on God to back them up.

But the next Letter has a different, and disillusioned stance.

Letters, Ex-Convert, Beecroft. I made a "decision for Christ" at a Billy Graham meeting, and never meant anything more sincerely in my life. I went away with a sense of having died to a former self, a worthless thing that I had formerly cherished, and with having been reborn to a new power and victory that seemed to promise infinite possibilities. I was 29 years old at the time and well educated.

It was not very long before a split began to occur between the very real experience I had had and the teaching and doctrines which at the time I had swallowed with it. Having kept my mind open and been prepared to learn as much as I could in the past five years, I discovered that the supernaturalistic doctrines that Dr Graham and his like believe in are simply the last remnants of an ancient superstition that has hitherto been more or less effectively tied up with real religious experience, but it is now being finally forced apart from it.

We are in a situation rather like that of the ancient world, where the old religion was dying (Greek myths, etc.) and nothing had come to take its place. Modern supernaturalistic believers are like those of the common people who for centuries clung to the old myths long after the more educated community had given them up.

I also found that the Churches, to which I hopefully turned in order to learn from people with the same experience as myself, were stocked with the ignorant, the self-deceived, and the simple-minded, well intentioned ones whose religion and way of life effectively cut them off from the experience of life which would have made them wiser.

I still believe in my "experience," because it gave me a new spiritual health. But I cannot, without surrendering my integrity, believe in the Christian doctrines and Churches.

Letters, Rev Douglas Taylor, Penshurst. As another minister I am also interested in this matter of the effects of the Graham crusades, and especially in the views expressed by the Rev Lindblom.

The great need of the majority of people today is not the kind of emotional outpouring that Mr Lindblom advocates; people have had more than enough of it. They do not want any more heat; they want more light. And they are not getting it from the Churches today. That is the answer to Mr Lindblom's question, "Why have we lost the majority of seekers who came forward for salvation in the great crusades?"

There are two aspects of the human mind, the affectional side and the intellectual side. Both must be satisfied. The theology and religion represented by the Grahams big and small is over-rich in emotional appeal, but almost destitute of satisfying intellectual fare. Until that lack is met, we will continue, as "Ex-Convert" says, "in a situation rather like that of the ancient world, where the old religion was dying (Greek myths, etc.) and nothing has come to take its place.

My experience is that there is a great demand today for really satisfying, penetrating answers to such questions as these: "What does happen when we die? How does my life here affect my life here-after? Will I meet my departed friends again immediately, or will I have to wait till doomsday? How does the life of religion make me happy for ever? How does religion give you peace of mind? Who is the God we are supposed to worship? Are there really three Divine Beings or just one? How did Jesus become divine? If Jesus is divine, can there be any other Divine Being? Was the suffering on the Cross really the whole of Redemption? How do we know what the Lord wants us to do? Is the Bible really God's word? If so, how do you explain some of the horrible stories in it? What do you mean by charity, and who is my neighbour? How do I get more faith?"

The list is almost endless. But answers are available, and when the Churches begin teaching them they will not lose "the poor in spirit," that is, those who want to understand.

Comment. Were the crusades effective? The churches do not keep proper records of various aspects of their congregations, so that there are no data-based conclusions to be made.

So, lacking those, it seems we might fall back on fact that the various Churches have now been offered a re-visit by Graham and his team. They have given the matter separate deliberate consideration but have all declined. So that means that they think such a tour is not worth the many costs involved. I think, however, it is not clear-cut. It is a fine balance. I suspect that if they had more money to spend on luxuries, they would be quite happy to indulge themselves with another visit from Billy.

RETARDED CHILDREN

The sad case of the murder of the disabled small child by his father in Western Australia brought forth many comments. It raised the issue of what actions can be taken by parents placed in the situation of having to care for a lifetime for such children.

Of course, one logical course open is to murder them, to wipe them out. The arguments against this policy and its many abuses are too obvious to bear repetition here. Can you put them in appropriate homes? Well, maybe. Sometimes in 1964 they were available, and sometimes not. Can parents get home help? Almost certainly not in 1964. In any case, will this continue for the lifetime of the child? And then, how is it for the parents living day after day with the child? Or without it, for that matter? Any way the parents turn, only hard choices confront them.

Letter-writers had something to say here.

Letters, J Jackson. NSW does shamefully little. It makes no provision for retarded children below the age of nine, though their need for training begins much earlier and those who are most experienced know that these poor youngsters are trainable and should commence training as early as four or five.

The State's educational system dumps them at sixteen and makes no provision for them except incarceration in a mental asylum.

Private schools developed by devoted parents and staffed by dedicated men and women (mainly women) are attempting the Herculean task of providing mentally retarded children with the tender care to which these children respond so affectionately.

The children themselves in such well-administered organisations as the Sunshine Homes at St Leonards and Inala at Castle Hill, for example, do not feel "institutionalised." They enjoy the company of others similarly handicapped.

It is, no doubt, a heartrending experience for parents to realise that a child is retarded mentally. It is very difficult for them to realise that for the child's sake and for the sake of other children in the family the mentally retarded child is both better off and a good deal happier when he does not face the competition of children more advanced mentally than he, either as members of his own family or not.

Stupid, or at the best unthinking, people frequently attack parents who permit their mentally retarded children to attend such schools as I have named and cause much unhappiness. They say---"Oh, I could never send my child away from me!"

That is an easy but cruel attitude to take towards parents whose devotion to a handicapped child is sufficient to sacrifice their own natural feelings for the child's ultimate benefit. For it must be realised in the natural order of things parents are likely to die before their children until their ultimate death. This provision some privately endowed organisations are trying to provide.

During their lives many of the children can become capable of economic independence if they are trained in what have become known as "Sheltered Workshops." Here, retarded persons learn to undertake repetitive tasks surprisingly accurately and well. Of those who after training have become able to accept such jobs in industry, not one has been dismissed.

If the Perth case stirs the public conscience it may be a good thing, whatever one thinks of the means which were used. If people who are blessed with fine, healthy children could be more aware of the problem they would, I hope, do more about it, either by money or in kind.

Letters, Mrs O Davidson. At North Ryde Psychiatric Centre, where I am the publicity officer of the parents and citizens' association, there is a ward of 24 mentally retarded boys. It has been proved beyond a doubt that the majority of these children, given the proper care, interested medical treatment, and stimulus, can live happy and useful lives.

These boys, under the supervision of a dedicated male nurse, have built themselves a small workshop, and it is thanks to the doctor in charge, teachers and nursing staff that this workshop is a going concern with contracts to fulfill.

This small unit is an excellent example of progressiveness but, unfortunately, similar facilities are not available to all those children who require them.

The Health and Education Departments must start at once, not in the vague distant future, to provide adequate hospitals for those who need them, and training facilities for those who can live at home. If such facilities were available, there would be far less despair among the parents of these children, and no cause for the kind of neurotic thinking that killed Bernard Benn.

Letters, Mrs Renate Cowan. When a man, after several drinks, runs down and kills a pedestrian, he usually gets away with a manslaughter charge.

Why, then, this degrading farce of a man being sentenced to death for killing his mentally retarded child after being under a terrible strain for several years. Surely, a more realistic sentence would not produce a wave of infanticide of the mentally handicapped in our community.

When faced with the fact that one has produced an abnormal offspring the temptation to do what Dr Benn did is enormous, but only a very few succumb to it.

The temptation is even greater when one has lain awake night after night wondering what will become of one's child when one is dead and there are few surviving relatives to take a personal interest in him.

Letters, Mrs G Simpson. Once again an unfortunate parent, driven to desperation by the hopeless condition of his retarded child, has carried out a mercy killing for which it seems he will either be hanged or imprisoned for life.

It is surely time that some amendment was made to our laws to avoid such tragedies. It is not enough to have a law which states "Thou shalt not kill." Of equal importance should be a law stating "Thou shalt not compel to live." By the laws of nature hopelessly retarded children would inevitably---and properly---die, but we in our questionable wisdom insist that they must be kept alive.

When I was in hospital with my last child, a baby was born which was so badly retarded that it could not feed, move or even cry, and yet a constant battle was waged to keep this child alive. It was fed intravenously and given constant attention by nursing staff. To what end? Only to become an intolerable and hopeless burden to its parents and to the community.

With the frightening problem of world over-population staring us in the face, is it not time to amend our laws to allow those to die who should die? The question of mercy killing need never arise; we would simply be reverting to the just laws of nature, under which any animal mother lavishes her attention and care on her normal young, knowing by instinct that it is best to allow the weak and subnormal to die.

Comment. The WA State Government commuted Dr Benn's sentence to 10-years of hard labour. This meant that he would be gainfully employed. It seemed likely that he might be released after seven years. His wife gained employment at the University of WA as a tutor in German, the faculty that Dr Benn belonged to.

NEWS AND TRIVIA

Letters, D Davids. Your article "Japanese Employers Are Great Chaps" is in my eyes a most revealing one of the country looked upon by some of us as already being, or at least becoming, Australia's best customer.

The question is, cannot this information be used to awaken the majority of our employers, who apparently fail to see that we can hardly afford to lose 60,000 days of labour in one year, because of industrial disputes? I quote from the article: "Most of Japan's large corporations have never had a strike among their workers, their annual turnover of staff (among male employees) is less than 1 per cent and, no matter how relaxed the circumstances, a Japanese wage-earner never speaks of his employer, be it a person or a corporation, on terms other than those of respect, gratitude and quite startling affection. Some psychologists account for this (by Australian standards) unnatural situation by equating the role of the corporation in modern Japan to the role of the father of a family.

But are we right and is this situation unnatural?

What about trying this recipe out ourselves? Surely nobody can be content with the staff/management relationship in offices and factories in this country. It is two people in the ring of a boxing match, knowing beforehand that one of the two will always win. Instead, let us voluntarily try to use now, lest it becomes too late, the means we still have at our disposal, in order to ease living conditions of our workers towards a level as shown in this report of your correspondent or as experienced in many industrial parts in Western Europe.

Apparently it can be done in a not predominately socialistic country.

DOWN ON THE FARM

News item. Mrs Arnold of Wombill had a different day yesterday. She is the wife of the manager of a large sheep property, 420 miles south west of Brisbane. She was walking across a paddock to get a horse, when her 90-pound pet ram appeared. The ram was clearly upset and charged at her and knocked her down.

When she got up, it knocked her down again. It did this four times. On the fifth occasion, remembering growing up with her brothers, she twisted its neck, and bull-dogged it to the ground. She then sat on it.

The ram still remained aggressive, so all she could do was sit on it. She did this for two hours until her husband came home. Her husband said later "I did not argue the point. I cut its throat there and then"

Mrs Arnold suffered extensive bruising to the face, and a cut right hand. Some of her clothing was torn off.

News item, April 16th. The Federal Government decided today to defer indefinitely plans to fluoridate Canberra's water supply.

April 17th. Malaysia and Indonesia keep niggling at each other. It was announced today that Australia would be increasing its military aid to Malaysia. This consists of road-building equipment, a few helicopters and minesweepers. There are no combat troops included.

April 18th. Nikita Kruschchev turned 70 today. He was awarded the title of "Hero of the Soviet Union", a rare honour.

MAY NEWS ITEMS

Princess Margaret has given birth to a baby daughter. The father, Lord Snowdon, said "she looks like a super baby". The Royals still made the headlines in Oz.

In Sydney this week, **1,400 women bowlers held their annual week-long carnival.** At the end, they had a dinner-dance, which they attended in their white uniforms, and some wore the white hats. The only men present were the orchestra, which played throughout the night so **that the women could dance with each other.**

Britisher Donald Campbell is back at Lake Eyre. He is again trying to break the land-speed record, and the firm flat surface of Lake Eyre might be the place to do it....

He was here in 1959, and as his trials progressed he got close to the record, **but the rains came and he was washed out....**

News item, May 6th. In his first trials, he reached speeds of about 200 mph, but **cut through the surface of the track and damaged it.** It will take about 10 days to repair the track.

Firemen in NSW are locking away their brass helmets and changing to plastic. It is expected that these will be lighter, and offer better protection from falling debris. Also, **they do not conduct electricity.**

A few important industrial Tribunals granted **long-service leave of 13 weeks to employees after working for an employer for 15 years.** Federal and the State governments are starting to accept this new provision, and it is **expected to become a standard employment provision.**

Hollywood star, **Judy Garland is performing to packed houses in Sydney**. She is apparently wowing the audiences.

A quote from **an Irish tourist brochure**: Leprechauns, willy-the-whisp, puca, bean sidhes, and gruagachs abound in the many unspoilt parts of Ireland.

A quote from **the Mayor of Lane Cove**: People are so keen about trees and shrubs in this municipality that they souvenir them for their gardens when we plant them in the streets.

News Item, May 23. Judy Garland's tour of Australia ended poorly. **After a good start, Judy disappointed her fans by** being late for four performances, appearing bemused on stage, forgetting her lines, and giving very short and angular interviews. At her final concert in Melbourne, she was booed and catcalled from the stage….

On arrival at Hong Kong, she said by telephone that **she hated Australia and would never go back.** "Chivalry is not known down there. All they know is kangaroos. The audience in Melbourne got out if hand. It was a stupid fault on their side, and they were completely in the wrong" ….

On arrival at New York, she was rushed to hospital nearly unconscious, and **was reported to be in a critical condition**.

OUR WHITE AUSTRALIA POLICY

It was almost 20 years since the war had ended, and for some people, time had healed the wounds caused by the Japanese conduct at that time. At the other end of the scale, there were many who would never forgive. In between, there was a growing body that saw the Japanese variously now as trading partners, as people we could visit, as humans to be looked at through Christian eyes, or as a nation who was a menace 20 years ago, but had changed now.

We were **more tolerant towards the rest of Asia,** and so our White Australia Policy was gradually being eased generally. But when you put this nation all together, there was still an enormous range of attitudes towards Asians of any sort, and no consensus at all about how many of them we should make welcome or accept, permanently or even as visitors.

When it came to China, the situation was even more complex because they were tainted in many eyes by their complicity with Communism.

The first short Letter below wonderfully mixes up a number of different grouches, but he makes it clear that he is not prepared to give a hand up to the then-starving Chinese.

Letters, F Fordham. The current drive to acquire additional overseas markets for Australian produce **must not be extended to Red China**. We should not even contemplate assisting the economic build-up of a potential enemy.

Many of those who advocate trade with Red China are the very same ones who heaped derision on our Prime Minister and dubbed him "Pig-iron Bob" on account of his decision to allow the sale of scrap metal to Japan prior to the Pacific War. We don't want to trade with the Chinks now any more than we wanted to trade with the Japs before the war.

The second Letter presents a different side of the migration story, a side we rarely thought of.

Letters, Andy. Dr Rivett is reported to have proposed a policy of letting into Australian non-whites of qualified professional and trade classes together with skilled and unskilled people.

As far as the qualified professional people are concerned, I, as an Asian student in Australia, am sure most if not all **Asian countries cannot afford the luxury of allowing the same to emigrate in large numbers**. Even if some fields appear to be fully satisfied in some countries, there are daily advances in technique and more new people are needed for tomorrow. The same applies in agriculture, industry and health.

Moreover, the teaching profession is in a state of infancy in today's scientific age, and qualified men are a crying need. If one day the dream of having enough qualified people for agriculture, industry and health is achieved, **we in Asia still will be faced with the problem of insufficient teachers**.

Hence I fail to see how any qualified professional and trades men can come to Australia from the non-white world.

UNIVERSITY MAYHEM, MAYBE

On May 6th, the students from the University of Sydney were scheduled to hold their annual Commemoration Day Procession. This was often a fun-filled event where a procession of about 50 floats was permitted to proceed from the University for a distance of four miles, through the city, and down to Sydney's Circular Quay. The floats were generally of a satirical nature, and were often very clever. As the parade moved along, hordes of volunteers shook brass cans in the faces of spectators, and asked for donations to some worthy cause. The conduct of most students was always silly, and in most years, quite inoffensive.

This year, it got off to a bad start the night before when a harbour cruise of 1,200 got out of hand. When it returned to the Quay, six of them were arrested, 10 were treated for cuts from flying glass and two were admitted to hospital. Thirty policemen and six ambulances met the ferry.

This was a bad sign for tomorrow. **For the students**, they started the day with raised antagonism towards the police. **For the cops**, they thought that this was one of those inevitable years where there might be something that the Press would call a riot. So what they did was to move the procession along quickly, and at such a pace that the students claimed that it was impossible for their foot-soldiers to collect money. So hackles were raised all round.

When the procession finished, students spread through the city, and some got up to mischief over the next few hours. Some gathered outside the US Embassy, and chanted and held slogans demanding human rights for US blacks. The police tried to move them on and the usual scuffles broke out, and charges of police brutality were popular for while. Overnight, the Cenotaph was "violated" by a clothesline stretching from one end of the Cenotaph to the other, covered in women's underclothing. The line was fastened to a bronze soldier on one side and a sailor on the other. An old umbrella was pushed under the arm of the soldier. There were other incidents, and most of them were as severe as those reported above.

The citizenry of Sydney did not like what they read in the papers the following day. The papers were full of indignation for days in what was the biggest Letters barrage of the year. I can offer you only a small sample.

Letters, S. Stephens, MLA, Sydney. With the forty-ninth anniversary ceremonies of Anzac so vivid in public memory the desecration and sacrilege of the hallowed site of Sydney Cenotaph by Sydney University hooligans is beyond description.

The behaviour of this inhuman element raises the question of future entry to our universities in these competitive days. Hundreds of students who in their own homes and particularly in their schools have been taught the principles of good Christian living and the value of Australian tradition have missed out on entry in favour of this disgusting element.

Those responsible should **be expelled and drummed out of the seat of learning and higher knowledge and sent to gaol as an example to the community**. There are ample would-be students properly equipped to take their place instead of spending public money on types of no use, benefit or ornament in this state.

Letters, Tom Noetel, Engineering I. Today was our Commemoration Day. Its object was (1) to collect money for SACHED, the South African Committee for Higher Education, and (2) to give the people of Sydney the student views on certain subjects.

Both of these are worthy causes and in both cases the Police Force did its utmost to disturb the proceedings. Admittedly there were some hooligans on the ferry cruise, and if it was students who defaced the Cenotaph then they were also hooligans, but these were a minority and we are also ashamed of them. However, all other demonstrations and pranks were peaceful until the police arrived.

I would like to stress the damage done by the police to the Commem Day charity, SACHED. The police escort, itself unnecessary, ordered the procession to proceed at the unreasonable pace of fifteen to twenty miles per hour, which made it quite impossible for students going with the floats to collect money and keep up with the floats. This practically ruined half of Commem and didn't help student-police relations.

On May 6, 1964, the New South Wales Police Force shamed themselves.

Letters, A. K. As a returned soldier and a father of two sons and a daughter, I was shocked to read in the Press of the vandalism at the Cenotaph and the rowdiness and drunkenness on the ferry on Tuesday night.

Can you tell me that parents have any respect for their children if they allow them to do these things? Don't tell me that a parent in this age does not know something of what his or her son or daughter does. Or do parents not **care?**

Letters, D Shortland, Guildford. Let us cease to be amazed that university students could have louts among their ranks. Let us shed forever the idea that entry to such an institution automatically changes the make-up of the human being and suddenly instils concepts of social responsibility and everlasting decency.

In the main, the student who enters fulltime courses at a tertiary establishment is nothing more nor less than a schoolchild who chafes under the feeling that the imprint of the academic nappy is still fresh upon him.

Such a child has suddenly been released from the comparatively disciplined atmosphere of the school, having got to the university merely because he has been better able to cope with rote learning than his fellows. All at once he finds that there are none of the threats that he has faced for the preceding five years and he comes face to face with the other animal, "girl": he has the same desire to show off as his matted-haired, slouching, leather-backed, unguided roadhog of the suburbs. His only claim to fame is that he is often able to exercise his better stimulated brain-power to effect his destruction more artfully: the result is the same materially, but more offensive aesthetically.

Letters, I Harding. Before the post mortem on Sydney University Commem Day is magnified out of proportion into a Students versus The Rest feud, may one who is both ex-student, ex-Serviceman, and unfortunately, a city worker, offer a few comments.

As to the alleged near-riot, disruption of traffic and the wrecking of commerce, it seems students are to be denied privileges freely extended to others. Seamen, building workers, wharf-labourers and other trade-unionists are apparently free to have protest meetings and marches, demonstrations outside courts, Parliament, shipping offices and the like, without protest by the police or leaders of industry. Similarly, parades through the city are frequently constructed by various organisations, visiting bands etc, again without protest.

There seems to be no good reason why every section of the community except university students should be entitled to demonstrate and disrupt the city. Other great cities of the world, notably New York, very frequently hold parades and demonstrations without unduly distressing leaders of commerce.

As to the desecration of the Cenotaph, if this was done by university students, and they deny it, I suggest that honourable amends could be made and ruffled feelings soothed if the SRC were to donate a small proportion of the moneys collected to Legacy.

Letters, Surgeon. The usual post-Commem Day clamour is erupting in the newspapers and once again the whole of a generally intelligent, alert and responsible body of young people is being condemned as a body for the actions of an irresponsible few.

The State President of the RSL, Mr Yeo, is reported to have called students "educated louts." Mr Yeo's remedy is to cut out Commemoration Day and let students "run backwards and forwards in the grounds of the university and stay there."

Since graduating in Medicine in 1957, I, too, have objected. I object to louts who also happen to be ex-Servicemen descending upon hospital casualty departments on Anzac Day in stages of inebriation and physical trauma.

I could call the actions of these few men on Anzac Day irresponsible and could rightly say I objected to being abused and assaulted by them while sitting up all night suturing split scalps. I could condemn the whole ex-Servicemen's body for not controlling its members properly. I could also suggest that they be allowed to run backwards and forwards in Martin Place and stay there so they don't clutter up public hospitals "sleeping it off."

It is so easy to condemn, but if we must, let's not be so sweeping.

Comment. It was clear that most writers had their own views long before Commem Day. They already had their grouches and prejudices against uni students, the police, the Returned Servicemen, and hooligans, and the South Africans that benefited as the charity for this year. It was also clear that a small proportion of the students wanted punch-ups with the police, and on the other hand, that some few police welcomed the chance to rough up a scholar.

The people who reacted to the clothes line on the Cenotaph were I believe, really offended. They held that site as being sacred, and consider that there are plenty of other places for smart-alecs to be clever. Still, there was another point of view, put by a student apologising to those offended. "At any other site, a clothes line would not be noticed. It was important to us that our line and thus our placards, against American segregation, be noticed." **Sorry, old pal, no one noticed your placards.**

The NSW Premier, Mr Renshaw, summed it up at the end. "I don't believe in letting my blood pressure get the better of me during Commem Week." A Deputy Commissioner of Police added "I seen better riots at my Saturday morning football with the kids."

SAFETY DOORS ON TRAINS

Letters, V H Kelly, King's Cross. Last Tuesday a startled schoolgirl of nine years, who was carried past her home station on the North Shore line, jumped from the train while it was travelling at 40 miles an hour and was seriously injured.

Once again, parents are asking why NSW suburban trains are not fitted with automatic doors as in other countries to prevent this type of accident.

One seems to remember the Railways Commissioner, Mr McCusker, making a promise many months ago that suburban trains would be equipped with automatic doors. If this work is in hand, it is progressing at the speed of a snail, and while this neglect continues no one can truthfully say that the railway is the safe way.

Surely there is a responsibility, too, upon parliamentary representatives to press for this improvement.

Letters, J Moth. Another youth has been killed in a fall from an electric train. He is reported to have been standing near a doorway, taken ill, fallen to the floor and then to have rolled out the open doorway. Such an accident could not have happened if the carriage had been equipped with automatic closing doors.

Yet, at the present time, the Railways Department is withdrawing from service some carriages already fitted with automatic closing doors and converting the doors to manual operation. One such carriage is No. 4788.

So much for the railway being the "safe way," or any intention ever to make it so.

Letter, Commuter. I am reminded of a Letter I wrote 10 years ago. I wrote "Here's a novel idea. If you have an electric train, one thing you can do is allow the passengers to open and shut the doors themselves, and that means you can have passengers fall out of the moving train and be killed at will. Another thing you can do, is have the doors close automatically when the train is about to leave the station. The problem with this is that some people might get caught in the doorway for a second, but the clamps on the door can be made of soft rubber that allows such persons to pull free. Just as they were currently doing on buses and trains round the world."

At the time, a full decade ago, the NSW Railways were under pressure to fit automatic doors to carriages. In the long run, they decided against doing this mainly because of a recent tragedy in Japan. There, a carriage with automatic doors had jammed, a fire had occurred, the doors could not be opened and everyone inside had been incinerated.

At the time, many people said that such an event was avoidable, that engineering had reached a level of sophistication that there was no chance of it happening with the right precautions, that buses and trains world-wide were safely using modern technology to good effect. These counter arguments were to no avail, and auto doors were not introduced.

Here we are then, 10 years later, and it appears that nothing has changed. At times like this, I sit and wonder. Is it me who is mad, or is it someone else?

NEWS AND TRIVIA

Letters, M Allen, Thornleigh. So the Secretary of the Road Safety Council considers folk of 60 and over too old to be capable motor drivers! I do agree that people of that age should not begin to learn to drive, but anyone with 40 or more years up and who has grown up with the changes in roads, regulations and speeds can be and is a better driver than the young fool who have just stepped into the modern vehicle.

I cut my teeth on cone clutches, straight gearboxes, two-wheel brakes and pretty terrible roads in both city and country. Surely after 40-odd years I have learnt sufficient to give me another 10 or 12 years. I am not a Sunday driver, but every day.

Letters, Victim, Neutral Bay. After living in a ground-floor flat for 15 years I continue to be amazed at the inconsiderateness of top-flat dwellers in shaking mops, mats, etc., from windows. We even have had the experience of one tenant emptying the vacuum-cleaner bag out of the window. The perpetrators must realise where the dirt is falling, and to come home after a day's outing to find large balls of fluff at one's front door is annoying to say the least.

It might be a good idea if councils introduced a by-law prohibiting this really offensive habit.

Letters, Noel Howard Powers, Double Bay. There are more reasons than one why Sydney's international air terminal presents a second-rate image to the world at large, and for the sake of national pride let's hope the responsible authorities attempt to rectify the problem quickly.

I refer to the anomalous liquor laws prevailing in the "Walk-About" lounge, which permits late trading when an overseas flight departure is imminent, and which makes a mockery of this passengers' amenity by appearing to attract more "deadbeats" per square foot than all Sydney's combined sly-grog joints.

No one wishes to deprive bona fide passengers and their friends of the right to a "glass of good cheer" prior to departure for or on arrival from overseas. However, the blatant exploitation of this privilege by many undesirables and the lack of any police supervision makes farewelling one's friends on a late flight an uncomfortable and **embarrassing business.**

Letters, (Margaret McKendrick. Has there ever been any other function held in Sydney which could bring so much ridicule upon the members of an organisation as that held by women bowlers in the Trocadero on Wednesday night, and given front-page publicity by the "Herald"?

What is wrong with the city leaders of the NSW Bowling Association that they should devise entertainment in such poor taste for country guests? How pathetic to see this fine body of sportswomen asked to attend an evening function dressed in "mutilated" bowling uniform, black shoes with white frocks, hats or no hats by choice, and even an odd piece of jewellery, and then to complete the fiasco by including in the program old-time dancing for an "all women" function. What would these same women think of their menfolk if they celebrated important occasions with all-male ballroom dancing?

It is to be deplored that an association of 38,000 should hold a function which makes its members the laughing stock of public opinion.

Donald Campbell is having trouble with his land speed record attempt. On May 15th, he had to pull up at 320 mph because of vibrations in the Bluebird that made him almost blind. He is getting the feeling that his team might not be able to get the track smooth enough for the record.

Cracker night. The newspapers were full at the moment protesting about the availability of fireworks. A week or so before Cracker night, communities were being unsettled by explosions, and dogs were protecting their tails as best they could. The volume of Letters suggested that at some time in the near future, governments might somehow limit the sale of crackers to the general public.

JUNE NEWS ITEMS

June 2nd. **Ringo Starr collapsed in London** yesterday and was taken to a hospital and kept there for an uncertain period. What a disaster. This means that **the Beatles tour of Australia might be postponed**. It is due to start in a week's time....

June 6th. Ringo will not be fit to fly with the other three Beatles in a few days. **He still hopes to join them in Adelaide for their first concert.** He has tonsillitis.

Australian jockey **Scobie Breasley** won **the English Derby** on Santa Claus at Epsom.

June 13th. About **200,000 people c**rowded the city of **Adelaide** as a formal procession welcomed the Beatles. There were no incidents, the crowd just screamed. And screamed....

June 15th. **Another 250,000** welcomed the Beatles to **Melbourne**. First came Ringo Starr, then later the other three. Lots of screaming, about 150 teenage girls collapsed and were taken to emergency casualty stations, and then all miraculously recovered. At a later press Conference, the Beatles said their welcome was their wildest ever, anywhere....

The first concert at Melbourne's Festival Hall went well despite hundreds of girls trying to invade the stage, a fire hose turned on a mob trying to enter via a back entrance, dozens of young men trying to gain entry via the roofs of buildings, hundreds of girls fainting again, and policemen sent sprawling. **Good clean fun**, and there were some reports **that music was also played,** though no one seemed to notice.

The cost of building **the Sydney Opera House** has blown out **from 3 million Pounds in 1957, to 17 million now.** It is expected to be finished in 1967. Maybe.

The Beatles scored again in Sydney, and were mobbed, and were again deafened by their audiences. On Saturday night, a boisterous but orderly crowd capped off the celebration of Paul's twenty second birthday **by raining the stage with jelly babies as birthday presents**....

The Beatles continued to impress with their clean-cut image, good manners, and **the (rare) ability of such entertainers to talk....**

10,000 screaming and sometimes sobbing girls said goodbye to the Beatles at Sydney airport. Some sank to their knees to join in the wailing pleas of "Don't go, don't go" and **"No, No, No"**....

It was a great tour, and I bet a number of my readers were among the screamers.

June 24th. **Prime Minister Menzies** was in New York. This afternoon it was reported that **he had died.** He quickly said the report was wrong, and that it was just an unsubstantiated rumour. Further enquiries proved this to be the case.

Regulations are starting to be announced for the new TAB agencies. It has been decided that no seats will be allowed on the premises, and races will not be broadcast in them. This will discourage punters from loitering.

A POST SCRIPT ON SELF-CLOSING DOORS

I would like to add a few Letters to the mix on putting automatic doors on trains. You will remember that I thought they were a good idea, and that everyone else should think so. Well, it turned out that not everyone did, and one person's view is worth considering. I enclose it below, with an irreverent rejoinder.

Letters, L Henry. Lately there has been a good deal of criticism of the Railways Department because of the absence of automatic closing doors on trains. For my part, the automatic doors are a nuisance and delay the loading and unloading of passengers. It would appear that the critics are reflecting teaching of the head shrinkers – that no one has any personal responsibility and someone else is always responsible for what happens to them.

If children are old enough to travel on trains on their own, they are old enough to be told, and to understand, that they should not stand near doorways. If they disobey – and fall out – they are in no different position from children who are injured or killed crossing a street without having observed the rules. I don't notice any suggestion that cars should be abolished.

In the case of adults, one has seen them push on to a train so already overcrowded that there is room for only a toehold, with body bowed outside the line of the carriage walls. Such a person deserves anything that may befall him and sympathy should, perhaps, be confined to his lack of mental capacity.

Letters, W Watkins. I would like to commend L Henry for his letter which I believe contained the best piece of downright commonsense I have read for many years. The idea that the authorities should forget about safety doors on trains, because stupid people who stand too close to open doors deserve to fall out, could well be applied to many other walks of life.

Stairways in future can be built without banisters, ships without deck rails, lifts without doors, miles of hand-railing on the Sydney Harbour Bridge can be dispensed with, as can in fact any safety devices whatever for responsible, sensible people over the age of six. Cars, of course, will no longer need horns, braking systems can be modified and seat belts not even thought of, on the principle that foolish people who drive at all fast deserve to be smashed up. Red lights, except outside doctors' surgeries, or on Christmas trees, will become extremely rare and we, the sensible, intelligent people like L Henry and myself, will live contentedly in a world free of such nuisances as safety devices.

Millions of people who are stupid enough to be elderly, incapacitated, too young, or who just lack the cool, steady self-control and the iron nerve of L Henry and myself will suffer from their stupidity and eventually become extinct. L Henry and I will not, however, waste any sympathy on them, as they deserve anything that may befall them.

SOME DAY I'LL WISH UPON A STAR....

Judy Garland got some bad Press from her time in Melbourne. Yet, in Sydney, she left behind many fans who were delighted with her. It is worth while letting a couple of them be heard.

Letters, Birdy, Burwood. The juvenile behaviour of the Melbourne audience almost from the moment Judy walked on stage until the end was thoroughly disgusting. Judy needs the audience to be on her side. Melbourne wasn't, and that was the whole trouble. In Sydney we laughed, cried and cheered until our throats were dry, but most of all we opened our hearts and loved her. This was all she needed to give us in return such an exciting and artistically rewarding performance that I was prompted to make the trip to Melbourne just to see her perform once more. But there I was confronted with an audience which would just not accept the fact that the joking, the talking and the incidents with props, are just part of Judy Garland being Judy Garland.

So don't blame Judy for a disappointing Melbourne show, blame the audience which seemed determined not to like her. Maybe the man who called out, "Act your age, Judy!" should apply his statement to himself and the rest of the so-called Judy "fans" in Melbourne.

Letters, A Lawrence. There can be no doubt that one reason why the Melbourne audience was not "with" Judy was that Sydney had her first. Anyone who understands the narrow Melbourne mentality must realise that such a situation as that was not to be borne by the dour inhabitants of the southern city, who are supremely jealous of Sydney and everything we have that they haven't.

That is why Sydney rarely sees the presentation of any theatrical show first. Most of the Australian premieres take place in Melbourne because theatrical management of long experience knows that for Sydney to be given preference means that Melbourne just doesn't want it. For that reason, the promoters should have presented Judy Garland in Melbourne first. It would have been a different story if they had.

First comment. It seems that Judy's life was like that all the time. Some people loved her, others did the opposite. Her illness in New York was by that time part of a pattern where she often sought medical attention, and many people thought that this was drug related. She died in 1969, at the age of 47, and again drugs were mentioned. In any case, love her or not at this stage, when the world first saw her in the Wizard of Oz she was truly lovable, and that is how most people, me included, like to think of her.

Second comment. The second Letter above reminds me of the rivalry that existed between Melbourne and Sydney in 1964. It had been greater in the past. Remember, 100 years earlier they had both been independent colonies, 1000 miles apart, with different laws, customs, and aspirations. The rivalry persisted after Federation, and was decreased by the two World Wars, and by the transportation revolution, and the increasing mobility of the population. But it persisted in a modified form up to 1964 and beyond, and it came out clearly here.

THE DEATH OF RADIO DRAMA

It my unpleasant duty to announce the death of an Australian institution. Let me explain.

Radio since the 1930's had carried two forms of entertainment that had affected the lives of millions of listeners. Firstly, there were the radio serials. Over the years there were dozens of these, syndicated over networks, that each came on for 15 minutes in the evenings and acted out diverse stories to an enthralled nation. Shows like Dad and Dave, Martins Corner, and the unforgettable Yes What? The Search for the Golden Boomerang was one I would never miss. At a time of no TV, and before the kids went to bed, most families tuned in for an hour or more Monday to Friday on the box with flickering lights in the kitchen.

Sadly, **this** institution went the way of TV soon after it started in 1956. Radio serials could not compete with Gunsmoke and Paladin in the new world.

A **second** radio **institution** survived, however. **This was radio dramas.** Here a play of some sort would be acted out on air, by local actors, using a script that was specially written as a one-hour play. Typically, each play lasted for an hour, and used well-known actors. Though, having said all this, some plays were spread over a few days, maybe even a week. In any case, they were much loved by housewives, who could do their chores with their transistor radio by their side, with a box of tissues standing by in case.

This brings me to my sad announcement. The radio stations somehow got together in 1964 and said they would stop producing these dramas. They would be replaced by "music for teenagers". This was a nasty shock for the industry that had grown up about this activity, but as I am sure someone said at the time "That's progress."

One final thought. The ABC never had many radio serials. One that it did have beat them all. It started out in 1944 as the Lawsons, and changed over to Blue Hills in 1949. It ran continuously till September, 1976. This was a total of 6,100 episodes.

The list of actors who played various parts over the years read like a Who's Who. Queenie Ashton spoke the first words in the first episode and the last words in the last. In between, others got a word in. These included Ray Barratt, Lola Brooks, Neva Carr Glynn, Anne Haddy, Nigel Lovell, John McCallum, John Meillon, Max Osbistin, Gwen Plumb, June Salter, and Rod Taylor.

One final point. The Lawsons started at the behest of the Oz Government in wartime. It wanted our farmers to produce more soya beans, and it thought that an appropriate farm-based radio programme would do better than straight-out propaganda. So it approached a lady called Gwen Meredith to write such a story, and away it all went for 32 years.

THE NAZI PARTY

In the middle of the month, the ABC aired a *Four Corners* programme that showed a 10-minute investigation of the Nazi Party in Australia. This was a purely Australian version of Hitler's machine, and copied its uniform, swastika, and its philosophy in full. It was dedicated to the preservation of the white race and white supremacy, it denied the persecution of the Jews, and it regarded Hitler as a hero.

The Party had its headquarters in the middle-class Sydney suburb of Ashfield, and had a membership of 270 and growing. Its leader, Arthur Smith was a balding, tough nut, well spoken and educated, and thoroughly rational. The Party intended to achieve political power by peaceful means.

The ABC producers said they worried about providing publicity for such a movement, but considered that it was proper that the nation should be alerted to what they saw as a threat.

There were plenty of writers who agreed with them.

Letters, Alexander Sills, Pendle Hill. The disadvantages resulting from the "Four Corners" report on the National Socialist party of Australia by far outweigh any possible advantages. A small group, having just started on the lunatic fringe of "politics," cannot possibly hope for better publicity than that provided by *"Four Corners."* It would take this party years of undisturbed and sustained efforts (and a lot of money) to become as widely known as they have become overnight, thanks to the ABC. No doubt the reporter had a very worthy intention to "expose" the Australian Nazis. However, he failed completely to contribute to this aim. The "exposure," if any, was achieved by the inherent wickedness and stupidity of the movement itself.

Instead of speaking of administratively organised mass murder, the interviewer used the Nazi phrase of "final solution of the Jewish question." When the prospective Australian "fuhrer", in answer to the question about the murder of 5,000,000 Jews, glibly replied that there were not as many Jews within Hitler's reach, the interviewer failed to ask the obvious follow-up question, whether it was all right to kill a couple of millions less. Neither did he mention that the Nazis did not confine their killings to Jews but exterminated many more millions of Russians, Poles, gipsies, etc.

This is written not to advocate doing nothing and closing one's eyes, but to state most emphatically that reporting such as this is most definitely not the way to combat Nazism, not in Australia or anywhere else.

Letters, H Rosendorff, Nedlands, WA. Instead of protesting against the "Four Corners" television program showing the activities of the pro-Nazi organisation in Sydney, the NSW Jewish Board of Deputies should be thankful that the ABC had the courage to expose the activities of this dangerous and un-Australian group of Fascists.

Don't say that 250 people are not dangerous. Hitler started **with fewer and it led to a world war.**

Letters, E Clay, Manly. "Four Corners," by featuring the activities of the Nazi Party in Australia, showed to viewers the naked face of unutterable evil.

While the existence of this party in our country is an insult to all those millions who fought and died that freedom might survive, it is nevertheless right that viewers should have the opportunity of seeing this feature.

However, in view of the fact that many of our young people have no personal recollections of the war which Hitler launched upon the world, and the dreadful realities of his "final solution," this film should be been accompanied or followed by an equal footage showing statistics of the enormous cost in human lives, and also some of the scenes in the extermination camps when the victorious Allies finally relieved the few poor human survivors of that terrible ordeal.

Letters, Ruth Sriber, Edgecliff. Like H B Newman, president of the NSW Jewish Board of Deputies, I loathe all that Nazism stood and still stands for. But, unlike Mr Newman, I think the segment on last Saturday's "Four Corners" program on the National Socialist Party of Australia was a courageous piece of reportage.

Certainly I didn't for a moment feel that it was propaganda for the National Socialist Party, but rather a devastating exposure of the aims and ideal of these so-called human beings.

If there are rats eating away at the wiring, let us all know and do something about it. If they are ignored and left to work quietly away, the lights might just go out again one day in the future.

Comment. As far as I can find out, a couple of National Socialist Parties tried for political office in the 1970's, but with no success. They appear to have faded away except for the occasional small groups of skin-heads with their leathers and motor bikes, who pose as Nazis without any knowledge of what it all stands for.

THE GOOD LIFE IN AUSTRALIA

A Letter to the *SMH* by a Peter and Shirley Arnold raised some interesting points. It is too long to quote in full, but it appears they are a couple, initially from Britain, but now living happily in Australia. They appreciate the very good life we have in this country, but worry that we might be **too** laid-back.

They talk about the pleasant and likable personality of the Australian generally, but criticise his preoccupation with closing times, horses, footy, and the like, and his lack of concern with education, foreign relations and immigration.

"Democracy has in a sense gone wild. Airline pilots strike, transport drivers strike, wharf-labourers strike, postal sorters strike. One would think that the country is in dreadful strife that all these men have to strike for their basic human rights. How far from the truth can one get! When will the Australian realise that he does not need an increase in the basic wage, an extra quarter-hour for tea, or the innumerable fringe benefits? When will he realise that life does not consist solely of beer, bets, sport, telly, and sending his children out to earn the basic wage as soon as possible?

They go on to ask why he is so little concerned with the fact that we live in Asia, and should be conscious of that inescapable fact. They conclude with the suggestion that we needed to take a less frivolous view of the world, and think about broader issues than we currently do.

Comment. Their Letter brought only a subdued response. Normally, criticism of Australia gets a lot of Letters, but not this time. I suspect that their mild tone played a part in this, but more important, it was because most Aussies agreed with them, up to a point. I will quote one Letter that spoke for most respondents.

Letters, Slim Williams, Heddon Greta. The Letter from the Arnolds is perfectly correct in all of its observations, and only in its conclusions is it faulty. We Australians do spend much of our time on folly. We know we are lucky, we are aware that others do not have it as good as we have it, and we also know that we do not have to spend our time in solemn, defeated communities going over and over our grievances.

There are communities all over England and Europe that are so downtrodden that they think having a good time is sitting round in the evening in squalor whinging about being alive. Here we can only think about serious things for a little while each day. Just ten minutes say. We can't see why we can't spend the rest of our time on the really silly things in life, if we want to.

What if we spent more time on education, or foreign relations, or immigration? Would we achieve anything? Do we have that much power down in our back yard? Don't we elect people to do that for us?

So, in summary I say that we are not the fun-loving idiots we might seem to be. Every one of us has his serious side, and can produce it when necessary. In the meantime, let us have our fun. If you want to have fun some other way, you are welcome. Or if you want to be miserable, please yourself. We will continue, though, on with our own harmless antics.

NEWS AND TRIVIA

Letters, Bridget Gilling, Castlecrag. The article on "Roman Catholics And The Pill" reports the Church as objecting to contraceptives in general, and the pill in particular, on the grounds that they violate the law of nature.

The law of nature appears to decree that hair shall sprout from the faces of men, that human beings shall not fly, and that human skin shall become dirty; but we interfere with impunity.

That only the fittest shall survive is also decreed in the law of nature. Yet the children (unwanted in many if not most cases) of the poverty-stricken, the syphilitic, the sufferers from the grossest of hereditary mental and physical disorders are cared for and shielded from the rigours of nature in many instances by devoted agencies of the Roman catholic Church itself.

The welfare of the human race depends to a large extent on preventing the conception of children for whom loving parents and adequate physical and mental health cannot be expected. **Selective use of argument from the laws of nature** by the Roman Catholic Church seems calculated to produce the greatest possible human misery.

SOUND ADVICE

Letters, Loyally Guarded, Balgowlah. In view of the increasing number of prowler attacks on women recently, I suggest that wherever possible all women who live alone, or spend much of the day alone, should get a watchdog. A dog gives the alarm when an intruder enters the gate, thus giving the householder time to lock the front or back door before answering the bell.

ADVICE FOR SMOKERS

Tobacco-product sales had dropped 30 per cent since the smoking-cancer scare. Now they are almost back to normal. There has been some switching. Many women have gone to dainty cigarillos. Some men had switched to king-size filters and cigars and long-stem pipes and chewing gum.

PITCHED OUT

A woman disrupted services at a Baptist Church in Los Angeles by deliberately singing off key. This was after a disagreement with her pastor. Yesterday a Superior Court judge barred her from attending services at that church in future.

JULY NEWS ITEMS

The Federal Treasurer, Mr Harold Holt, has announced that **the nation has done well during the financial year just finished**. He had previously expected that we would have a deficit, but now expects a small surplus. Happy days are here again.

Indonesia and Malaysia have not settled their differences. Every day there is some variation on their position, one day advancing, the next day withdrawing, the next day getting sulky, and the next day beaming goodwill. That is the same on both sides. All the while, the Brits and Americans and a host of other nations are proposing this and that, and being considerable nuisances. **If anything of substance happens, I will let you know.**

Dean Dixon, **the Musical Director of the Sydney Symphony Orchestra**, will conduct **a concert for 4-year-olds**. He will play small sections of various compositions of classical music. The children will sit with the orchestra in the body of the hall, and **be free to touch the musicians and the instruments**. Dixon concedes that if the sessions get too chaotic, they will have to stop before their allocated 45 minutes is used up.

North and South Vietnam are becoming a hot-spot for the world to watch. Recently the North, with a so-called Vietcong Army, won victories over the South in the Mekong Delta, and seem to be inclined to go after some more. America is getting restless about the southward expansion of Communism, and **Australia will need to keep pace with America**. Watch this space

The US Presidential election is coming up on Melbourne Cup Day. Barry Goldwater has just become the official candidate for the Republican Party.

News item. **Donald Campbell crashed through the world's land speed record yesterday.** His average speed, over two runs, of 403 miles per hour broke the previous record of 394 mph. He left the Lake Eyre track strewn for seven miles with pieces of rubber from one of his tyres that slowly disintegrated during the run.

There are now 38 shopkeepers who have not paid their fines for late trading, and are **expecting to be sent to gaol forthwith**.

Donald Campbell will lead a procession through the streets of **Adelaide** to mark his success on Saturday. **He will travel at 10mph.**

July 24th. If you want to go skiing, this is the weekend to do it. The snow at the moment is the best in years.

July 26th. The Sunday Telegraph reported **savage racial riots in Rochester, USA**, with 2000 black rioters and 700 police. Severe looting also occurred.

The US will send another 5,000 troops to Vietnam. That will bring **the number of "advisers" there to 15,000**.

In the **Fourth Test match at Old Trafford** in England, Australian captain **Bob Simpson scored 311**. Australia won the series one to zero, after rain washed out four matches.

THE PILL IS COMING

About 1956, the first large scale trial of the Pill found that it worked pretty well, and since then it had been improved and trialled, and by now, it was really starting to come to market.

It was too early to see its effects. Would it have side effects, good or bad? Would it free women for a life of promiscuity? Would Catholic women be sent to Hell if they used it? Would if affect a woman's fertility? Would the population drop if it was used too much? There was no way at this stage to answer such questions.

CARE OF UNWED MOTHERS

You won't be surprised when I tell you that this is not a new topic. Somehow it seems to keep coming round again and again, and for some reason it seems to be world-wide. Here, in our secluded island, I last had a major look at it twenty years ago, in 1944, and when I look back, I can find several major differences. Let me elucidate.

Of course, the causes are well known, and so too are the consequences and the choices. Discussion in society has always been about who is to blame, what can be done about it, and how do we stop it in the future. On the way, there are all sorts of arguments. For example, some will argue with the word "blame", and say that "blame" implies guilt, and that the girl is not at all guilty. Another example is to argue that "what can be done about it" implies it is like the measles, and that there must be some sort of cure for it.

Others will say it is all caused by failures in the home, and by delinquent parents. Or, by failures in the schools, or society, or outside agencies in that they do little to educate girls. Some will say boys should get their share of blame, and responsibility, and education and the like. Others will say that in that case, the boy deserves to have some say in the decisions.

Now, the matter has again hit the Press, I can see that there has been a large increase in the assistance available, but even more evident is the change in attitude to the mothers themselves. The most obvious change here is that blame was then, in the past, much closer to the surface, and that now the level of stigma has been much reduced.

Let me ramble on with an example from 1944, 20 years ago. I remember a number of Writers to the *SMH* who advocated that "hard core cases" should be sent to country Homes, and there **have their heads shaved** and work at the Home till their hair had re-grown. This attitude, **that you had sinned, that you deserved to be punished, that you must repent**, was all too typical of the day. This was an attitude that was often found in society, but also was found in many of the religious institutions, and in many of the clergy, that were catering for the young girls.

I came from a country town of 2,000 people, and left there to go to University in 1952. At that stage, I could tell you the names of all the girls, and their partners, who had conceived out of wedlock. I could also tell you the names of all the bastards that I had gone to school with. The point in my ramblings now is that in earlier years, there was a huge stigma attached to births outside marriage, and that punishment, perhaps for life, was part of the deal.

As I read the Letters in 1964, it seemed to me that things had changed very much for the better. It was clearly true that the physical arrangements had much improved. Adoption agencies had become more professional, organised foster care was becoming available, medical advice was more readily available and more affordable.

Importantly, attitudes were in the course of changing. Look at this Letter below. Of course, it is a puff piece, designed to put the best possible light on what was now becoming an industry. But puff piece or not, it would not have been possible to write it 20 years earlier.

Letters, Joan Burch, Horsnby. According to a report in the "Herald", the Rev Alan Walker spoke of the lack of facilities for unwed mothers and announced that Lifeline intends at a future date to open a home to accommodate women who find themselves in this situation.

The problem of the unmarried mother is not a new one and there are at present six homes caring for these girls and women. They are staffed and maintained by the Anglican, Catholic, Presbyterian and Salvation Army Churches and some of the homes have been in existence for over 50 years.

Anyone who has had contact with the homes cannot help but be impressed by the work that is done by dedicated and devoted staff members. Not only is the physical health of the girl cared for by adequate medical attention during pregnancy and the birth of the baby. There are also either resident or visiting social workers who help the unwed mother in the difficult decision she must make as to planning the best future she can for her child. Through warm understanding the often lonely and unhappy girl is able to regain her self respect and be better equipped to face life after she leaves the home.

Of course, the fact that the criticism and stigma was decreasing did not mean that it had all gone away. Here are a few current thoughts on the matter.

Letters, Fair Play, Neutral Bay. While congratulating Mrs Joan Burch of Hornsby on her letter, in which she pointed out the creditable work being carried out by the six homes maintained for this purpose, may I take exception to the phrase "the often lonely and unhappy girl is able to regain her self-respect" as a result of the warm understanding, etc., she receives at the home.

Now my point is concerned with the assumed loss of self-respect. In these days of teenage morality or loss of it, is it not time our social laws were revised? Should we not now remove the stigma from the unwed mother in view of the fact that so many of our young people frankly indulge in sexual experience, but are sufficiently worldly wise to take precautions against becoming "unmarried mothers"?

It appears to me that the unmarried mother may, in her innocence and undoubted ignorance, be the victim of society, indeed of hypocritical and self-righteous society, which itself indulges in the very same experience, quite frequently, for which it condemns her.

Let us be done with this farce and help these girls without such patronising verbiage. Let us remember that to most of us the sin is only in being "found out."

Letters, (Mrs) H Gould, Cronulla. "Fair Play" has obviously had little to do with welfare work among unmarried mothers, since his or her "point is concerned with the assumed loss of self-respect."

Let me assure "Fair Play" there is nothing assumed about it. Often the most difficult task is in restoring a feeling of pride in the unwed mother and a sense of balance. Fortunately for this society, there are many who are not similarly "found out" who also feel a tremendous loss of self-respect for having sinned, and seek help from their respective Churches to find a new strength of spirit to overcome their sense of guilt.

Sin is sin, and always hurts someone, so ours is an unhappy society indeed if we truly believe that the only crime is in being found out.

Would "Fair Play" alter other laws also, so that the unlucky few who get caught daily need not feel victims of a "hypocritical and self-righteous society"? Often one gets caught, and the partner in crime goes scot-free – does that make one less guilty than the other? Should society throw all the Commandments overboard because of this?

It is not the law that needs altering – it was given as a firm basis on which to build a happy, healthy society. Society needs to look up and live up to the law – God first, others second, self last – therein lies love.

Letters, C Hirst. The general tone of "Fair Play's' letter would seem to imply that it does not matter how young people behave morally, and that we should alter our social laws to suit them. This attitude is difficult to understand, when the majority of parents and guardians are doing their utmost to help their young folk to have an ideal and to respect themselves and their friends of the opposite sex.

Letters, Ian Harvey. Recent discussions in the "Herald" dealing with the relationship of the unwed mother to society indicate not only that there is a general failure to understand the basis of this social problem but, with many, also a total unconcern.

If we are prepared to face the problem from the right end, we can see that the first positive need is that children should be taught from the earliest age the unique value of family life, which includes the respect of, and acceptance of responsibility towards, every other member of the family, as well as the true measure of love.

The examples set by devoted parents should not be underestimated in their effects, nor should the damaging effect of domestic disunity, particularly between husband and wife, be ignored. Furthermore, the parents' privilege in home training must also involve imparting to children an adequate concept of God as well as an appreciation of basic Christian principles.

Hand in hand with family training goes an adequate sex education. This must first be established in the home and, if necessary, supplemented by community teaching both in the schools and as provided by church and other qualified agencies.

Dealing specifically with the problem as it exists however, two things are clear. First, there are inadequate facilities in the way of hostels and homes as are now provided by some Churches to a limited extent, notwithstanding that there may be adequate medical facilities provided by the State. Secondly, the Christian church, because it is qualified to deal with the basic needs of people, has a unique contribution to make in this field and should be supported wholeheartedly by the community at large as it seeks to provide human understanding, Christian love and expert help in dealing with the unmarried mother.

Letters, E Knox, New Farm, Qld. None would dispute Ian Harvey's contention that the best solution to illegitimacy is its prevention, but until we have a society of completely mature people, imbued with the Christian ethic, soundly educated with regard to sex, and with full insight into their own emotional needs and those of others, single girls will still become pregnant. In truth, few of us measure up to these requirements.

However much one might like to think that the Christian Church is qualified to help with this problem, one must question how expert is the help given to unmarried mothers in some maternity homes run by the different church organisations?

For instance, how many maternity homes employ trained social workers? What of the homes that refuse admission to the girl in her second pregnancy? What of the homes whose policy is that a mother should feed her child for as long as six weeks before parting with it for adoption? What of the home that extracts, before admission is arranged, an undertaking from the pregnant girl that her babe will be adopted?

And what of the maternity home which is also an adoption agency, purporting to place babies in good Christian homes, provided they are perfect specimens? Don't babies with congenital deformities warrant good Christian homes?

While appreciating that some church homes do excellent work for unwed mothers, anyone with experience in this field knows that the others exist in this country. Do they in fact "provide human understanding, Christian love and expert help in dealing with the unmarried mother"?

Many fine words are spoken in the name of Christian charity, but one begins to wonder how much is sheer sentiment and hypocrisy.

Letters, Mother, Middle Cove. Ian Harvey's letter brings again to my mind the over-emphasis placed on the phrase "sex education." What we need is "moral education" – it is necessary to teach one's children not only the facts of procreation but also the restrictions and self-control demanded of them by our society and our Churches, and the sorry consequences of lack of that control. Mating is instinctive – control must be learnt and forewarned is forearmed.

"Give them knowledge and keep them busy" is as good a maxim as I know for helping the young over those difficult developing years. There are so many good things to learn.

Comment. For some reason, I suspect that this is one problem that will not go far away. Still, maybe the increased usage of the Pill will change everything. We must wait to see.

ARE THINGS BETTER IN SPAIN?

We all know that there are all sorts of problems with unwed mothers, and sexual activities among our young and not so young. Would it not be nice if someone could wave a wand and suddenly they went away?

Well, here below we appear to have such a wand. It seems that it will take a bit of discipline, but it looks like we will end up with a much better society.

Letters, Worried Future Mother, Sydney. I have just read the report about the sex criminals and really it is terrible how many there are every day, I do not think it is so difficult to stop many of these crimes.

I come from Spain. There we do not hear anything about these things. They do not happen very frequently. You may ask why? I can tell you. Everything starts with the children. For example, you can go to a park, beach or cinema, anywhere, without the spectacle of girls and boys kissing each other – or something worse – in public. You are not allowed to wear bikinis on the beach, or these terrible topless dresses.

Now you will ask, how can they stop this? The answer is "penalty." In each park, beach or cinema there are policemen who can fine the boy instantly, if the boy refuses to pay, then both the girl and boy go to gaol a day and a night. This is the penalty for kissing in public, but, if children are watching, the penalty is much greater. Incidentally, a girl is 23 and the boy 21 before they are at the age of consent. So you can see why they behave and there are almost no illegitimate children there.

There are not many separated parents either. But in cases where parents separate, the children are taken and put into boarding schools and only allowed out three or four days at Christmas time until the age of 14, boys, and 16, girls. This may sound very strict but we did not have the trouble in Spain as here.

Sounds pretty good. But wait on a minute. Here are two other Letters that cast some doubt on what otherwise appeared to be a good thing.

Letters, One of the Pursued, Maroubra. I don't doubt that "Worried Future Mother" came from Spain, but when and why? Her verdict on "terrible topless dresses" might surprise the gendarmes in the more remote parts of Spain. As for bikinis, I wore mine on every beach along Costa Brava down to Alicante and along the Atlantic coast. I have heard the people in the far south are far more provincial and narrow-minded.

My views weren't formed during a hasty tourist trip, but over a period of many months living and working in the deeply religious and moral countries of Spain, Italy and Greece. In each of these countries the average man was absolutely lecherous. The Greek attitude, probably due to his heritage, is far healthier than the Italian or Spanish.

Prohibition has never prevented anything. The Spaniards keep their own women indoors after curfew and during the day they are well protected by the family, so when the "foreign women" arrive it's open season. The only Spanish women around to witness such manoeuvres are the more broadminded or travelled and the "loose" women of the oldest profession.

I am a respectable and responsible citizen but I couldn't reveal here some of my experiences in these religious and "moral" countries. Also, I taught English to teenagers and heard quite pathetic stories of how they escaped from home for an evening rendezvous ... nothing spared. Attending evening English classes was a wonderful excuse.

Letters, Liz Smith. I have not visited Spain, but a number of my friends have in recent years enjoyed the pleasures of that tourists' paradise. They all reported on the inadvisability of women travelling alone or even in twos in Spain, because of the unwelcome attention of Spanish men, who, denied the pleasure of kissing Spanish girls in public, force their attentions on foreign women in the streets and particularly in crowded public transports.

NEWS AND TRIVIA.

Oh goodie. I have the space to present some decent trivia. There is no particular theme. Just odd things of interest.

Letters, H Howe, Pymble. At the age of six weeks our Border Collie pup developed an interest in TV programs. Whenever livestock appeared on the screen he would take up his position in front of the set with the obvious intention of heading off any sheep or cattle which broke away from the mob. Then came the Beatles whose performances interested him intensely-

--he would stand up and attempt to lick their faces whenever they appeared on the screen.

On the Beatles' departure he switched his interest to teenage shows. At the end of each program he went into fits of tail-chasing which became so frenzied that eventually we took him to a vet, who diagnosed tranquiliser pills---which proved very effective.

The dog, however, developed a taste for them. Whenever one of the family moves along the verandah past the cabinet in which the pills are kept, he follows, sits in front of the cabinet, and, as plainly as a dog can, asks for a pill. When he doesn't get it he shows every sign of extreme annoyance. Is he becoming a tranquiliser addict?

Letters, Eric Gash. The Test series against England has concluded, rather appropriately, by drowning. Let us leave it as that and make no further efforts to breathe new life into this doddering, decrepit anachronism, this carryover from a bygone age.

With it, let us submerge beneath the engulfing waters the host of radio, TV and newspaper auxiliaries and their inane phraseology. Let us also submerge those batsmen whose scoring prowess is eulogised and immortalised should they produce an occasional burst of over 10 runs at the rate of a run every three minutes, and whose reputations are further enhanced by a muddling century once in every three or four years. With them go those negative bowlers who are too cunning to bowl at the wicket and be hit. If they can't be hit, neither do they take a wicket.

Subtract all these from present-day cricket and we have nothing left but the Ashes. These could be suitably disposed of by sprinkling them over the last watery resting-place of cricket, thus providing a fitting epitaph for its demise.

Letters, Jack Bassett, Bexley North. The rather pretty be-flagged "179" badge on late-model Holden cars seems to have an irresistible appeal to some schoolboys!

Thousands have been levered off bootlids in recent weeks, usually with damage to paintwork and sometimes (as in my case) to the steel lid itself. Trying everywhere to replace mine, I was told that a schoolboy (not named) had 80 for sale at 2/ each, all stolen from cars.

A spare-parts dealer told me that police who questioned boys at a school recovered 140 of the badges. But car damage is the real worry. Couldn't we have an eleventh commandment in the new religious syllabus, "Thou shalt not meddle with motor cars!"

PROBLEMS WITH RAPE CASE

Justice Collins, in the NSW Criminal Court, suspended hearings against four young men for nine days. They had been charged with rape. The Judge said that community feeling against rape had been heightened by two well-publicised incidents in the last few weeks, and that it would be difficult to empanel a jury that had not been affected.

GET OFF THE COUCH

A Mr Ormsby, Letter-writer, wrote to the *SMH* to say that every man up to late middle age should be able to walk 50 miles a day, and run a mile in 8 minutes….

"All too many men in the older groups find excuses for soft living and failure to exercise."

AUGUST NEWS ITEMS

There was a pronounced lack of interest in **Wattle Day, August 1st.** Twenty years earlier most children **wore a sprig of wattle to school**, and classes did essays related to wattle. The main reason for its demise, it was said, was that **it brought on hay fever**. Also, with the growth of the suburbs, wattle was no longer easy to get in the city. **"Lots of children haven't even seen wattle"**.

American Scientists from NASA were able to take **photos of the surface of the moon from a rocket** for 17 minutes before it crashed into the Sea of Clouds. They said that this will open up a new era in astronomy and space research….

The *Sun Herald* showed **a few pages of photos** that were taken. They looked very much like the small craters taken on earth. Doubtless they meant more to NASA scientists, who really were excited about them. The most significant thing revealed by our own papers was that there were no little green men.

The *SMH*, in a Feature article, asked how **Japan had come to be our biggest customer in the year 1963-64**. I checked, and found that it had just pipped Britain…..

The *SMH* marvelled at this. Japan adhered to an enigmatic philosophy, spoke an incomprehensible language, did not play cricket, had no James Bond, and had sent no Captain Cook or Ned Kelly to help shape our past. We had been aloof from it for a century, except for three years of military hostility. What had we done right?

Vietnam is getting hotter. The US is now raiding torpedo bases in North Vietnam, in retaliation against some retaliation. It is also building up its forces in friendly nations round Vietnam. The President is making those dreadfully serious "Addresses to the Nation". **Keep watching.**

Ian Fleming, the author of the James Bond series of thrillers, died in a Canterbury hospital at the age of 56. It is interesting to note that he had earlier formed himself into a public company, and more recently announced that he had sold 51 per cent of himself for 100,000 Pounds to a sugar and investment company.

The Minister for Defence is **considering imposing National Service on Australia's young men again.** In other words, he thinks that the situation in Vietnam and Malaysia is getting to the serious stage. He probably also thinks that **the Army needs a bit of a shake-up** before it will be ready for combat.

A Mr Thomas Allen, a Sydney shopkeeper was sent to gaol of Tuesday for not paying a fine. **He died later in the day, whilst still in gaol, from a heart attack.....**

That night, **a police guard was place of the home of the Minister for Labour and Industry.** He was responsible for administering the shopkeeping laws. This was after a number of angry phone calls had been fielded by various authorities.

Two days later the Government said that **its policy was still to goal persons who did not pay fines.**

JUSTICES OF THE PEACE

There had been a few minor complaints about the role of Justices of the Peace. It turned out that these were not justified, but the problem arose because they were being asked to perform acts that they could not legally do.

The Chief Secretary for NSW, Mr Kelly, took the opportunity to point out to the public some of the functions and duties of a JP.

Letters, C Kelly, Chief Secretary, Sydney. The article dealing with justices of the peace creates an impression of the role of the JP which is totally unfair both to the Government and to the men and women who carry out the duties of the office most conscientiously.

It is true that there are many thousands of justices of the peace in New South Wales. There is in fact a full list of them maintained in this department. Officers of the department have been complimented frequently and in particular by members of the legal profession on their speed in checking names of persons who have signed documents as justices of the peace.

Although there are many thousands of persons appointed as justices of the peace, it appears there are still not enough. This department is continually being asked by members of various professions and by businessmen, as well as from time to time by members of Parliament, to recommend further appointments to fill a need in particular places. These requests come more from the country areas than from the city, and they are evidence that the appointments are not to be considered trivial.

The judicial powers of the JP are governed by the Justices Act administered by the Minister of Justice. These powers have been greatly reduced with the establishment of stipendiary districts which have provided full-rime trained magistrates throughout the State. The justice of the peace performs a most important function in our legal processes and, however it may be styled as undignified by some, it is a function upon which all citizens place a great reliance and which must be available freely at all times and in all places.

Every nomination for the appointment of a justice of the peace is examined carefully and a full police report is obtained to establish that the nominee is a fit and proper person to be appointed.

My Department supplies to every justice on his appointment a brochure setting out in simple terms the duties and responsibilities of the office, and information is also made available on literature of a more detailed and technical nature which may be obtained. I may add that the officers of this department are always available to give advice or guidance to any justice of the peace as to the performance of his duties.

Comment. I remember in Hawaii in 1990. I had just been appointed to lecture at the university, and part of the rigmarole was to approach a JP (a Notary Public there), get an appointment three days hence, and submit to a ten-minute interrogation regarding my history, and then swear allegiance to the President of the US, and then be issued with a letter saying my application had been seen by the notable. The whole thing cost $50. Need I say that the Notaries **there** are paid officials.

In contrast, here in Oz, I need to get something like a will witnessed by a JP. So I ring at 7 o'clock at night, he tells me to come round when I like, and he checks my identity, and signs my document. There is no fee, and no fuss, no one is self-important.

Our Australian JPs, **all volunteers**, have been doing this since before my childhood. They do it for free, they seek no glamour, and they make themselves available at the oddest hours. They are an institution, and the Chief Secretary's words could have gone much further as far as I am concerned.

NED KELLY IS STILL MAKING NEWS

Australians have always found it hard to make up their collective minds about Ned Kelly. To some, he was a likable rascal, who thumbed his nose at an overbearing authority, who also was prepared to take from the rich. Though, it must be said, not much inclined to give to the poor.

To others, he was a criminal, he broke the law, he was a robber of hard-working men and honest businesses, and in the end he was a violent killer of policemen. An out-and-out outlaw.

He was back in the news this month. The pot was stirred by a well-known artist Sydney Nolan in an interview on the BBC, in which he spoke approvingly of Ned. I will let the Letters present a typically garbled picture of the life and times. .

Letters, C Gardner, Newcastle. I have long been exasperated – and no doubt others are also – by the growing tendency to beatify the Kelly gang.

I am a native of the "Kelly country." To my grandparents and their contemporaries the end of the gang was "good riddance to bad rubbish"; my parents and their contemporaries were thankful that these and other local menaces such as Morgan and Bluecap need no longer be feared.

I write this letter because of the disgust and derision with which I heard a remark by the artist Sydney Nolan, in a broadcast of "The BBC Calling Australia" on August 1. According to Mr Nolan, his sainted Ned, with his usual daring, held up a country newspaper office and "dictated the story of his life to a linotyper" (sic). The blessed Ned departed this life in 1880. The linotype machine was not patented until 1884.

Closer examination of the rest of the now widely propagated "Kelly legend" would doubtless bring further similar rubbish to light, and show Ned Kelly and his gang simply as the thieves and hoodlums they really were.

Letters, M Cutts, Mona Vale. Like C Gardner I have long been infuriated by the hero-worship of Ned Kelly. I personally regard him pityingly, as an under-privileged delinquent and his bravery as psychopathic bravado. He hit the headlines by reason of nuisance value. Is this a character to make into a national image?

His legend has been an inspiration in Australian art and literature. I applaud these arts, but deplore that a criminal should be their hero.

As in the case of C Gardner, I have every right to feel offence. I am a very old Australian. My great-great-grandfather and his brothers were pioneers and had to battle with life in a new land, which was hard enough without the depredations and violence of bushrangers. Ned Kelly was not around, but the "Jew Boy" gang once held up a store owned by one of my great-great-uncles. An employee at the store was shot dead as he tried to escape to summon help for his master and the latter's young son, who were held prisoners and in danger. His bravery is commemorated by a small monument, at Scone, NSW, set on the approximate spot where this gallant young man was murdered.

Australians with pioneer blood cannot fail to feel resentment that a national hero is fabricated from a criminal – or criminals, if we require more of these "heroes." It is no doubt true that many bushrangers were unfortunates, more or less driven by desperation into crime. But does this set them above those unsung pioneers who struggled lawfully and toiled like beasts of burden on the land?

Letters, R Mathews, Narrandera. My father was born in the Kelly country, and was about 15 years of age when Kelly was hanged. He was an intelligent professional man and university graduate, and I will never forget how he told me, as a schoolboy, that Kelly was more sinned against than sinner, and that he was driven and persecuted to commit murder.

All critics of the growing legend should read the proceedings of the Royal Commission held to inquire into the Victorian Police Force, soon after the Kelly episode. The fact is that we have a convict heritage. On this foundation, assisted by the atmosphere of the goldfields and incidents like Eureka, we have built a solid dislike of policemen. The present generation does not seem to have this, but nineteenth-century Australia did.

Until he shot the policemen at Mansfield, Ned Kelly was no more or less than a horse stealer. The three policemen who went to arrest him were going on the evidence of another policeman who had given perjured and lying evidence against Kelly. Kelly knew that he would be brought in probably dead, rather than alive. The Kelly family had experienced long and prejudiced persecution by the police. When he shot the policemen, Victoria knew that he had to hang, but all Victoria was still on his side for the simple reason that all Victorians were against policemen.

The police force of the day, in Victoria, was recruited from adventurers, remittance men, freebooters, ex-Army personnel, and so on. It was untrained and badly led. Read the Royal Commission report.

Ned Kelly was never a common bushranger. By shooting the policemen at Mansfield he unconsciously expressed what most Victorians felt about the police force of the day.

He was a brave man, whatever else he was, and had he been born about 1896, I have no doubt that he would have been decorated on the beaches of Gallipoli.

Letters, Odd Trick, Sydney. Whatever may or may not be the truth regarding the Ned Kelly legend, there is no doubt that its continuous survival is largely the result of the amateur set of armor which this man made for himself. Without this gimmick, rid of his iron mask and chestplate, where would Ned Kelly stand today?

Letters, S Edwards, South Curl Curl. I was in New York a few years ago, and entered a lift in one of their skyscrapers to go to the twenty-fifth floor of the building. The lift-driver was an Irishman.

I was wearing an Australian Air Force Association badge in my coat lapel and the lift-driver spotted it and asked me what it was. When I told him he remarked, "So you come from Australia, do you? You're under the British out there, aren't you?" I replied, "No, we are not under the British; we ARE British."

This conversation ensued:

Lift-Driver: The British are the greatest thieving, murderous race that iver lived.

Me: I don't agree with you.

L.D: They pilfered and stole from ivery country they iver wint to.

Me: I don't agree with you. They gave us a very good start out in Australia.

L.D.: Indaid, they did nothin' of the sort; it was the Irish that did everything that was iver worth doin' for your country.

Me: Did you ever hear of Ned Kelly?

L.D.: Indaid I have, and a foiner man ever lived.

Me: (with the lift door open to facilitate a hasty getaway):

Well, we hung the b------d.

CALL FOR NATIONAL SERVICE

It was not a coincidence that as the world around us was getting more warlike, advocates for militarism were becoming more obvious.

Letters, Rex Becke, Defend Australia League, Turramurra. The announcement by the Minister of Defense that the Government is considering the introduction of National Service training and strengthening of the Services generally is very welcome.

Over the past few years Australia has talked big and entered into various security arrangements which she could not possibly honour because her words have lacked the support of military strength. The Defend Australia League has consistently advocated: (1) A realistic scheme of National Service training for all three Services (two years' full-time service); (2) the immediate replacement of the obsolete Canberra bomber with modern, long-range strike aircraft, capable of hitting at enemy bases; (3) the urgent need for a modern attack aircraft-carrier to give the RAN a more aggressive role.

WE'RE IN THE ARMY NOW

When I was writing a couple of earlier books, I did a fair bit of reading on the Army. I was swotting up on two famous Australian soldiers, Sir Thomas Blamey and Gordon Bennett, and the role they had played in and after the war. One thing I learned was that between the two World Wars, the Army had nothing much to do. So that the numbers of soldiers of course reduced, and defence spending fell, and morale dropped to a very low level. When things started to hot up again, with the approach of WWII, a lot had to be done to rectify the situation, and in particular the calibre of officers still remaining left something to be desired.

In 1964, there had been some rumblings in the Press that the morale of our Army at the moment was dropping to an unsatisfactory level. After all, since WWII and since Korea, we had fired few shots in anger. We had taken in a few large batches of National Servicemen, but no one could claim that these reluctant soldiers were likely to improve the morale of Army regulars. So, it might be that things were not too good in uniform.

In August, a curious conversation broke out in the *SMH* about the Army. I almost classified it as Trivia, but re-thought it. If I want to use it to answer the question of how morale in the army is going, I can't. It is too superficial, and indeed it scarcely touches on the subject. But in a curious way, it does tell you something about what and how the Army is thinking, and whether its officers are right up to scratch.

Letters, G Meredith, Brigadier (Rtd). I read with considerable interest the criticisms of Major W

Burnard, about the standard of officers. It is comforting to know that there are still officers on the active list with sufficient intestinal fortitude to speak the truth, however unpalatable.

The Canberra "brass" takes a very dim view of anyone who has the temerity to speak unpleasant home truths, consequently it is practically certain that in the not so distant future Major Burnard will find himself placed on the retired list. If and when that happens, it will be the Army's loss.

The statements of the Director of Army Public Relations that "the standard of Army officers was never higher", is arrant nonsense. The Army is thousands of men under strength, the percentage of men who re-engage is shockingly low and, to cap it all, over 100 officers, or about 20 per cent of the total officer establishment, want to resign. These things just don't happen in an efficient organisation.

My only criticism of Major Burnard's article is that he breaks the golden rule laid down by the late General Sir Brudenell White – "never offer mere destructive criticism – if you cannot show how the things you consider wrong can be corrected, say nothing." Major Burnard does not say how this matter can be rectified.

There is, I submit, a simple solution. Restore to officers' messes the dignity and tone of prewar days. Officers' messes today are merely places where officers have cheap meals and drinks. Since the war, there has grown up the bad habit of officers drinking in the mess bar: while doing this they frequently discuss confidential matters in the hearing of the staff. All drinks should be served in the ante-room and drinking in the bar forbidden. The general standard of dress is deplorable. I was lunching in a mess recently and a man walked into the dining-room and sat down. He had his sleeves rolled up to his biceps. He was a major.

After retreat, the only dress allowed in themes should be mess kit, evening dress or undress blue. Dinner should be a "parade."

Letters, Ian Hamilton, Mosman. Brigadier Meredith is quite right. If the Army would restore to officers' messes the dignity and tone of prewar days, the Army would be the better for it: officers would be gentlemen again.

In a further attempt to save the world from destruction we might also rebuild the British Empire: after all, any trouble with the Ruskies or the Heinies or the blacks was easily stamped out in the days of Empire, and look how peaceful the world was.

Let us also put the lower classes back where they belong. So much money and leisure has taken away their proper humility before their betters. We should remove the vote from women and make them our obedient servants again. We must send a gunboat up the river to call on the heathen Chinese in Peking, and as for the dastardly Indonesians, if the Dutchmen won't colonise them it is our painful duty to do so.

Gad, Ponsonby, the world is going to the devil, sir!

Letters, "B" Echelon. No former member of the AIF can fail to agree with Brigadier G Meredith's views in support of recent criticism of Army officers and senior NCOs and also with his suggestion that dignity and tone should be restored to officers' messes as a cure for current ills.

It was indeed rare that a lance-corporal was heard to swear in the lavish junior NCOs' messes maintained throughout the siege of Tobruk. And it is actually recorded that an Australian sergeant (and holder of the MM) broke down and cried at seeing a second-lieutenant from a British artillery regiment drinking from a water bottle in full view of two captains from the Free French Army and a Polish staff officer.

My father, who served in France with the 4th Australian Division, advises that sleeves were never rolled up on the Somme front unless wounds were actually being dressed. The use of chipped enamel mugs by ranks above WOII rendered offenders liable to Courts-martial.

Letters, G Jamieson. Brigadier Meredith's letter endeavoured to show that there is something radically wrong with the Australian Army. It was apparent that he revealed aspects which should be eliminated if it is to be restored to full efficiency.

This was evidently not the impression made on Ian Hamilton, who, in an endeavour to ridicule this viewpoint, introduced entirely extraneous suggestions such as dispatching a gunboat to Peking and rebuilding the British Empire.

There can be no question of putting the lower classes back where they belong but it appears obvious that to have discipline in the Army (and an army must become a rabble without it) certain standards must be fixed and rigidly observed. Time was when a button left undone could lead to fatigue drill. Standards must have sagged seriously if a major, who should surely set an example, is allowed to enter a mess for a meal in such a state of undress as was described in Brigadier Meredith's letter.

Many people would strip our law Courts of the standards and procedures which have ensured the administration of justice as well as can be in an imperfect world. Eliminate the dignity with which the Courts are conducted and we will see the farcical scenes which a part and parcel of American Courts.

So it appears to be with the Australian Army. Evidently many things have drifted and we are indebted to Brigadier Meredith for bringing this drift under public notice.

Letters, Ex-Sergeant, Woollahra. Ian Hamilton's cheap gibe at Brigadier G Meredith's letter about the Army misses the point. The brigadier's letter concerned Army discipline and deportment – not ways to save the whole world. We may yet need that discipline and deportment the lack of which the brigadier deplores.

Comment. To me, a humble private, with only National Service experience, it all seems more formal than the army I remember.

CLEVER YOUNG MEN

Two young men using bows and arrows have killed 28 wild pigs in the last two weekends on a property at Moree in rural NSW. They could not shoot them with a rifle, because the noise "shooed them off". The arrows use three-foot shafts with two-and-a-half inch tips.

LIMITS ON MIGRANTS

European nations are making it difficult for their citizens to migrate to places like Australia. They are worried by the outflow depleting their working population. Spain has just introduced restrictions, and that leaves only Britain and Holland who have not moved to place limits.

SEPTEMBER NEWS ITEMS

The American Aircraft carrier, **USS Enterprise**, will soon visit Sydney. **It is nuclear powered**, and has a length of 1,100 feet. That is about 17 cricket pitches. It has **a crew of 4,600 men**. About 1,200 visitors' tickets will be issued for each of the two days the ship is in port.

India has asked that four grain ships going from Australia to Britain should be diverted to relieve its critical food shortage.

A Japanese trade representative, Mr Kawanishi, said that **silk shirts, slacks and suits will make a comeback**. Sales of silk to Australia have fallen from ten million Pounds before the war to one million pounds now. Japan started blending silk with artificial fibre two years ago. He expects most silk exports will soon be blended.

The Port Jackson and Manly Steamship Company will start to **use a hydrofoil** in the Manly run later this year,

The NSW Minister of Public Transport last night banned **the execution of U-turns in the city** of Sydney. They are still legal in other NSW cities.

It is reported by members of the NSW Labour Caucus that **the influential Chief Secretary is in favour of ladies' hairdressers staying open for trading one night a week**. "We are out of the bowyang era", he was reported as saying. He was also **in favour of opening cinemas for Sunday shows**, but the influential Theatrical Employees Union is opposed.

Prime Minister **Menzies has given up his 1949 Cadillac** which he has been using since 1949. It is **the oldest car**

in the Commonwealth fleet. He says that the firmer upholstery gives him greater support when alighting than modern cars. He is now trying out a Bentley.

Swimming Champion **Dawn Fraser** announced her engagement to a Townsville bookmaker only hours before leaving Australia for **the Tokyo Olympic games**.

The WA Minister for Development, said that he was considering **using an atomic blast to clear Geraldton Harbour of rocks**. He was having talks with a US group called Ploughshare at the moment, and he was hopeful, though he realised there was still a lot to do.

A newly registered company, Paris Distributors said last week that it planned to **sell contraceptives via vending machines** in NSW through clubs, night clubs, hotels and railway stations. Last night, the NSW Government moved to change the Factories Act to make **it illegal to sell contraceptives through vending machines**. The Minister for Labour said the move was in **the interest of public morality**.

On Saturday, 5th of September, if you wanted to watch TV, you could have started with **Abbott and Costello** in *Buck Privates*. A few hours later, you could have switched to *the Donna Reed Show*, then *Bandstand* for a while. Probably then *Sunset Strip*, or *Rawhide*. Finally, you would have finished up with a corny movie. Or you might have stayed up a little while longer to have a few minutes of religion at the close of transmission.

RELIGIOUS EDUCATION IN SCHOOLS

In August, the NSW Minister for Education, Mr Wetherell, announced a new approach to the teaching of religion in schools. Current practice was based on an Act of 1880, supplemented by revisions in 1959. He noted that many changes had occurred since the initial Act, and in particular that religion now did not permeate society as it had then, and that there were many more people who espoused no religion, and that also many people practiced religions other the Christianity.

He thus sought to change the syllabus and arrangements for religious instruction in State schools (only) and in primary schools (only). He aimed to create an examinable subject that would present **a broad overview of religions of the world**, including Christianity as just one of these religions. The fact that it was examinable meant that children could not opt out of it as some of them did with the current religious instruction. It was also envisaged that the Churches would be given time to push their own barrows to those of their own denomination who wanted to attend their sessions.

Mr Wetherell was being very brave here. He was in a Christian country, where most persons casually or seriously attended some services. The 1880 Act had given the Church of England certain guarantees that it valued, and which would have been weakened if the changes were introduced. On top of that, there was the vested interest resistance. Many clergy saw that if other religions were given a toehold with children, then they might think of going to another completely different religion.

The supporters of the new legislation thought that the move would increase understanding in a world that was getting more diverse, and that it was becoming necessary to mix with people of other cultures. Some of them also thought that it was not possible to argue that Christianity was the one and only true religion, given the numbers of people who thought differently.

At this stage, I will stop giving **my** breakdown of the situation, before I offend anyone else. Instead, I will present Letters from *SMH* readers, and hope you will believe that **I have tried to give equal time** to the proponents on **every** side.

Letters, Jim Russell. It is now 84 years since the enactment of this piece of legislation, and if young Australians are to grow to appreciate Australia's Asian responsibilities, then part of their social studies curriculum must be devoted to Asian studies, including Eastern religions. This should have its rightful place as part of general religious instruction, just as should the study of Christianity, as the traditional basis of our Western culture.

Letters, Ernest Vines, Narraweena. I believe many Christian people, as well as non-Christians, will welcome this syllabus. There is a great need for tolerance in the world. There is much good in other religions which should be recognised, even if Christianity is the best religion.

The NSW Presbyterian Assembly last May passed a resolution instructing the Theological Hall Committee to consider plans for more adequate instruction in comparative religion. This new syllabus does not propose instruction in comparative religion, but it does not encourage narrow dogmatism. It recognises that we ought to know something of the religions of our Asian neighbours. It stands for the highest in ethics and religion.

Letters, (Mrs) M Young. As the mother of a four- and five-year-old, I would like to endorse the new religious syllabus for NSW primary schools.

To those who, like myself, completed schooling 20 years ago only to Intermediate standard, the need which this syllabus will help to meet should be very apparent. Without any background knowledge, it takes years of trial and error, thinking and reading, to come to the realisation that for thousands of years people have been struggling for truth through study, thought and experience. The young mind should have been given an introduction to this type of information; it is essential to an all-round education.

Now children have the opportunity of hearing of every field of human endeavour, especially what has been wrought by religious and philosophical thought and the action which followed, as well as the plain fact that there is not only one school of thought, but that there are many of them. I do not believe this can be done by concentrating on one religion (in our case, Christianity). At present it is implied that the spiritual history of a pocketful of people points the way to the solution of all problems connected in any way with human life.

This syllabus is a challenge not only to Christianity but to all schools of thought – not to capture the freedom of the mind of children, but to teach them to work out their own salvations in the splendid company of all who have lived and learned since the dawn of history. If Christianity is confident that it has superiority over all other religious, moral and social bodies, it must be able to face the task of presenting all sides of the question, knowing that if it is superior, it will benefit most.

Letters, (Rev) Hunter Matthews. It is absurd for Mr Wetherell to suggest that the teachings of all religions amount to the same thing. Those who have been trained under tertiary disciplines in Divinity know how such statements can be a dangerous over-simplification. Admittedly, the many religious faiths among schoolchildren is a problem: but this is not the answer. If Mr Wetherell wants to make constructive changes in the present syllabus then he ought to **leave religious instruction to those academically competent to teach it adequately: ministers and religious leaders who hold qualifications in Divinity from theological colleges and universities.**

We do not wish to impose Christian teaching on non-Christian children. However, we must not expose children of Christian homes to a false generalisation which will be subversive of proper Christian training. This is what Mr Wetherell appears to intend.

Letters, Mary Haveron. The syllabus is an effort to bring this understanding to those who cannot or will not see the other chap's point of view.

I write to say that the Christian principles which motivated it should be plain for all who think clearly. Social understanding is imperative to all races in this sad world.

Isn't this the basis of Christian teaching? Didn't Christ teach this very principle, "Love one another"? Have the Christians followed His teachings? If so, why do we, who profess His teachings, fight and wrangle with each other?

Letters, William Revell, Sydney. Re your editorial, I am 100 per cent against any form of "general religious teaching" in schools, I stand firm on Christianity and

Christian principles, all emanating from the Holy Bible. I want no other. Is this a Christian country or is it not? No, sir. Let's do all honour and justice to her Majesty the Queen, as Defender of the Faith, by maintaining Christianity in this great country of ours.

Letters, (Mrs) Elaine Moon. I am disappointed by the hostile reaction of some clerics to the separation of general religious teaching from social studies in primary schools.

The two subjects are different. That God exists, or that Jesus changed water into wine, are beliefs that many able and respected men have challenged; and it is dishonest to teach them as if they were as widely accepted and seriously unchallenged as, say, that Blaxland, Lawson and Wentworth crossed the blue Mountains.

I do very much want my four children introduced to the Christian faith and tradition; but only in a way making it quite clear that Christian beliefs are opinions upon which it is both possible and permissible for people to differ.

Letters, L Irvine. The distinction between the functions of the Churches and the State in religious teaching seems to be a step in the right direction as it is clearly a matter for the Churches to teach the tenets of their own particular denominations, while the position of the State is different because it is made up of people of many different faiths and denominations, and should not put itself in the position of favouring any one of them in its teaching in the schools.

I think the introduction of the new syllabus is a liberal-minded move and should be encouraged.

Letters, M Miller, Beecroft. The rev Hunter Matthews would have religious instruction left to "those academically competent to teach it adequately; ministers and religious leaders who hold qualifications in Divinity from theological colleges and universities."

Having thus disqualified (I speak reverently) Buddha, Christ, Confucius and Mohammed, where do we go from here?

Letters, Eileen Ridley, McMaster's Beach. Are we or are we not a Christian community here in Australia? I and many others have always believed that we are. Then surely our schools are Christian schools and must remain so.

Why is it that so many people seem to be afraid to stand fast for what they believe, but are ready to back down or compromise at any breath of adverse criticism? The Bible predicts that there will come a famine, not of bread, but of the word of God. Surely that prediction is apt to be **fulfilled in our own time.**

Letters, Grace Kirkwood, Coff's Harbour. It is sad indeed to hear of young Buddhists and young Christians butchering each other in the streets of Saigon.

Perhaps if their primary education had included some studies about the good points in the beliefs of the other group, these tragic events would not have happened.

Letters, (Mrs) S T MacDuffie, Potts Point. The perfect answer will not come from your columns, but from the ballot-boxes in the next State election. As one who has lived in six large districts in NSW, including the Far West, I predict that the reply will be devastating!

Comment. Some of you will remember that religion was a more divisive subject back in 1964 than it is today. That is obvious from the many different opinions.

The last Letter, though, clearly has some merit. **The forces of democracy did have an effect**, because after four weeks of contention, **Mr Wetherell said that he would postpone the implementation**, and would have a new Syllabus Committee review his proposals. He even said that he might allow Churches to have representatives on that Committee. In the meantime, the status quo prevailed.

THE VOYAGER ROYAL COMMISSION

The Royal Commission into the collision of the Voyager and the Melbourne handed down its findings at the end of August. It said that the prime responsibility lay with the Voyager, because it did not keep a proper lookout, and did not make proper efforts to remain aware of Melbourne's location at all times. The Melbourne had some responsibility because it did not respond quickly enough to the threat of collision.

Two days later, Prime Minister Menzies told Parliament that no Court Marshall would be filed against any officer. He added that he had decided this, because any evidence provided at a Court Marshall was not subsequently allowable in evidence against them in civil or criminal hearings. This somewhat murky explanation suggests that Menzies knew of further legal actions that were pending. **This in turn suggests that we have not heard the last of this matter.**

REAL SIGNS OF REAL WAR

At the end of the month, I am afraid I must go back to talk of war. Most of the time when I am writing these Baby Boom books, I find that people are talking about a war somewhere or other and they tell me that it will be real bad, and that someone or other is the baddie, and of course their mates are the goodies. I generally follow the Beatles and their "yeah, yeah, yeah", and say that I am not convinced.

Most often, I get things right. I was wrong about the Cuba crisis, but I got the Korea crisis right, and had a lot of fun saying the Suez crisis was all talk. In any case, what I am saying is that I do not get apprehensive about a big war very easily.

So, it is with reluctance I have to admit that everyone is getting too warlike **in our part of the world**. The troubles in Malasia and Vietnam are rapidly taking on word-wide proportions, and the big players are moving armed forces and equipment and resources to that area.

In our own country, day after day, there is some front-page headline that seems to be **conditioning us to a war** coming soon. Menzies and his Minsters are talking about their anxiety, the Minister for the Army is complaining that the Army is short of men. He is also mumbling about introducing National Service, the *Sunday Telegraph* had a huge headline that said "WE COULD BE BOMBED" by the Indonesians. Even the Brits are sending combat troops to Malaysia, there has just been a military coup in South Vietnam, the Americans are whipping themselves into a lather about the Red menace. Like I said, day after day this type of news is inescapable, and it has me very nervous.

It is all backed up by an increase in soft news items that talk about war-like matters. Take these few Letters below.

Letters, David Scarlett. At a time when the state of Australia's defence forces could well be described as alarming and when there exists to the north an expansionist power apparently dedicated to military adventurism, I feel the necessity for the recent "Herald" agitation for an increased defence effort should be deplored.

The news itself should provoke action.

It is not enough for the man in the street to talk about our defence inadequacies. Something must be done and it is within the power of each of us to do something. Whether as an elector by writing to his local MP, or as an employer or parent by encouraging CMF service, or as a young man joining the Forces there is something we can all do.

Perhaps it is the effect of living too long in a tension-filled world which has robbed the country of an ability to see the present danger. Nevertheless, danger does threaten. It has been pointed out and appears to have aroused only apathy.

Letters, David Dale. How long will it be before Australia realises the necessity of **stockpiling nuclear weapons?** Before we start thinking of minor details like National Service, we need enough real force to be able to threaten the Indonesians with total destruction if they seem to be regarding our shores with an invasive eye.

Letters, D Watts. What the well-meaning supporters of these peace movements apparently do not realise is that the Soviet probably wants a nuclear war as little as do the non-communist peoples, but that she is fighting, and at present winning, a deadly ideological war. Since the invention of long-range weapons, a convenient propaganda base has become more valuable to her than a military base, and the creation of a propaganda centre more useful than a military victory.

It is very pleasant and brotherly for people of different nationalities to get together and exchange ideas and opinions, but the creating of an atmosphere of friendship and understanding among ordinary people will not prevent war. The brutal fact is that whether there be peace or war is determined by the heads of Government, not by the people.

I am old enough to remember how well liked and how very much admired were the Germans by the British people generally before World War I, and how that did not prevent the British and the Germans from going to war. Many people must be old enough to remember, and others near enough to the pre-World War II period to know, how helpless the very strong pacifist movements of the 1930s were to stop the outbreak of another war.

It is a good thing for the Governments of countries to come to an understanding and work out agreements that are advantageous to all; but then is the time to keep up a guard against ideological infiltration. Then is when people are apt to slip into the easy attitude that since the Russians or Chinese are good fellows, Communism cannot be such a bad thing; and it is well to keep in mind the sheep's clothing nature of much Communist propaganda.

So, I am worried that a bigger war in **our region** might be coming, and **that we in Australia will be dragged into it**. Having said that, I promise you I will not harp on it, and will only talk about it if something changes spectacularly. But I ask you to keep it at the back of your mind, unless I give you some type of all-clear.

NURSES DRAGGED THROUGH THE DIRT

Letters, Nurses J Harrison, A Eagleton, M Howitt, R Pilou and J Evans, Sydney. We are a group of nurses from a Sydney hospital who are united in outrage and indignation at the way in which, during recent years, the name "nurse" has been dragged through dirt.

The nurse of today is regarded by a certain sector of the community as being some sort of a cross between Florence Nightingale and a common prostitute. This is largely the result of a good deal of unnecessary Press publicity given to nurses. For example, should a typist be the unfortunate victim of assault, the news item would perhaps be titled "Girl Attacked in Park." But if the poor girl happens to be a nurse it is a different matter! Big, black headlines proclaim "Nurse Raped in Park." Please, we are sick and tired of this degrading and unnecessary emphasis.

There is not much we can do about this situation. We just have to put up with sidelong glances and insinuating stares from people in the streets. We are nurses. We expect cracks about "Little Florrie and her lamp" and even grow to like the cheeky but well-intentioned calls of "Nursie, come and hold my hand." But we will never get used to the comments of people who read day after day about nurses and who believe what appears to be written between the lines – that nurses are cheap!

Certainly we are not all paragons, but we would like to see the stigma that is developing around the word "nurse" removed for ever. We have our self-respect!

Letters, (Miss) H McKenzie, NSW College of Nursing, Glebe. The old concept of the nurse as a girl who serves a hard apprenticeship doing menial jobs and a bit of nursing thrown in has gone by the board. If it hasn't, it should.

As a result of the courses organised at the New South Wales College of Nursing, this image of the nurse has changed dramatically in society. The nurse today is trained not only to help the sick. She acquires skills and a thorough education that enable her to hold the highest posts in administration and teaching institutions if she wants a career.

Letters, Edna Peskett. I, as a matron of long standing, now retired, feel that their complaint is fully justified. However, this is only another manifestation of a far greater mcnace that threatens the sacred name of the profession.

I understand that it is now common practice in many hospitals to employ a high proportion of entirely unskilled and untrained women as nursing-aides, who, after three months' service, are permitted to don a cap and the title of "nurse."

In several cases known personally to myself, some of these women are incapable of maintaining their own homes and families to normally accepted standards of hygiene. How far short then are they of public hospital standards, particularly those relating to obstetrical wards, and the nursing of lying-in mothers, where regulations allow that only trained nurses should attend after delivery.

If the situation continues, it must result in a decline of standards and the public image of the profession.

OCTOBER NEWS ITEMS

A number of *SMH* readers are complaining about getting poor seats to live theatre shows even when they applied early. They said they had all written in early, **in legible handwriting and sent a self-addressed envelope and a cheque. How quaint.**

51 per cent of first-year students at Newcastle Teachers College **failed a spelling test.** So says Grif Duncan, the principal. The tests used words that were known to be commonly misspelt. He said that the proportion of bad spellers had remained **steady over ten years.**

October 10th. **The Tokyo Olympic Games open today.** Our girls will wear lemon-yellow dresses, deerstalker hats, bone-coloured Cuban-heeled shoes, and white gloves....

Missing from the parade will be our competitors in Monday's and Tuesday's events. This included all the swimmers. It was claimed that the parade would leave them exhausted....

Dawn Fraser was one of two girls that defied the ban. They were smuggled onto the bus as it left for the parade. She returned to their village aboard the bus, and as she stepped off, with a cigar in her mouth, she was cheered by other swimmers....

She later got herself into hot water by wearing **a swimming costume that was not part of the official uniform.** She said that her chosen costume was more comfortable, and that she swam faster in it. She was also one of a few Australian athletes that **stole an Olympic**

flag from the Emperor's palace, and she was arrested by Japanese police. They did not charge her. **More will be heard of this.**

October 11th. For the very first time, more than one man has occupied a space ship. **Russia yesterday put three astronauts into space**, and they are expected to stay there for at least a week....

The score in the space race for the year is now one-all, after the USA won a point for its photos of the moon a few weeks ago.

October 14th Dawn Fraser won a gold medal for her win in the 100 meter sprint. **It is the third time she has won that event.**

October 14th. **Joan Sutherland** opened the opera season at **New York's Metropolitan Opera** with a sensational performance that wowed the critics and the audience. **She took 20 curtain calls.**

Australia has now won two gold medals, and two silver and three bronze medals at the Olympics.

A half-Senate election will be held on December 5th.

Nikita Khrushchev has stepped down as Russia's Premier and First Secretary of the Soviet Communist Party. He has reached the age of 70. His health is faulty.

After the elections in Britain, **Sir Alec Douglas-Home will step down as Prime Minister.** The Labour Party won 316 seats to the combined likely total of the opposition of 314. Harold Wilson, as leader of the Labour Party has said that he will form a government despite his very small majority.

THE VOYAGER STILL IN THE NEWS

Commander Robinson, of HMAS Melbourne, was not found guilty of any offence in the collision, and was not subject to any disciplinary charges. Still, after the Royal Commission, his posting was revised, and he was offered the post of officer in charge of HMAS Watson. This was a land-based position, mainly used as a training facility and for administration. Such an offer was an insult to the commander of an aircraft carrier, and he resigned from the Navy.

His resignation was accepted, and morale inside the Navy plunged. Feelings throughout were bitter, and more will doubtless be heard of this.

RAPE ALSO IN THE NEWS

In fact, if you look for it, rape was always in the news. On this occasion, 10 young men had invited two young NSW girls into their cars, and taken them to a remote place, and most of them had raped a 17-year-old. A few of them were sentenced to life imprisonment, and others to periods like 10 years. Outrage in the community was great, and the soul-searching was profound. The first rash of Letters is given below.

Letters, G Furby. Every right-thinking and decent citizen will commend Mr Justice Collins for his sentences on the gang of rapers in Sydney Supreme Court on Thursday.

Gang rape should be made a separate offence with a minimum sentence of, say, 15 years upon conviction. Unfortunately, in the light of past experience, most of these criminals will be released by the Government upon the people after serving only a few years of their sentences.

To those who say the sentences were severe or harsh, I would say they were no severer nor harsher than what the rapers inflicted upon the innocent victim. Their enjoyment of life has been curtailed; her life has been completely ruined.

The sentences were imposed with logic and courage, of which more could come from the Bench these days.

To those female relative who allegedly screamed and yelled at the sentences, I would say: Put yourself (if you can) in the place of the victim, and then see what tone your screams would take.

Letters, William Revell. The sentences in the rape cases (life imprisonment) are, in my humble opinion, far too savage and unwarranted, although no one suggests the culprits should go scot-free.

It wouldn't be human if we never had some attraction to the opposite sex. But it is inhuman to inflict a life sentence on mere boys for this offence. I don't recall a life sentence imposed in Britain for rape (unless it amounted to murder).

We are not in a position to attack South Africa's oppressive apartheid unless we can show mercy to our own people.

Let us search our consciences, each one, asking ourselves our own feelings if it were a brother or a son.

Most Australians I have discussed the matter with say I am wrong. This leads me to wonder: Is the Australian callous by nature?

Letters, Citizen, Sydney. Few people will not be distressed by the facts of the recent case of rape in which 10 youths were involved. There will be widespread sympathy for the victims of such an atrocity and no doubt there will be general agreement that the Judge did his duty in imposing severe sentences.

This and other cases that have occurred recently, however, must also raise in the minds of thinking people the question of the extent to which society must share the guilt. Society, after all, has moulded these youths – or failed to mould them – to behave as they did. One wonders, for instance, whether their school education included in the curriculum such matters as problems of sex behaviour, a rudimentary knowledge of the law and the penalties for crimes. If it did not, does not some responsibility for this and similar crimes rest with our system of education?

To leave such matters to the discretion of parents is to ensure, in some homes, that they will not be treated at all, and in others that they will be handled very badly. Who is to say that neglect of these matters was not a major contributing cause to this recent tragedy that has brought ruin to so many lives?

Surely society is evading its responsibilities if it does no more than provide heavy penalties for rape. Much more must be done to search for and deal with the causes of behaviour that has such disastrous consequences for all.

Letters, Melbourne Visitor, Prahran, Victoria. While not in any way attempting to defend the crime of rape, I cannot altogether agree with the public outcry. There can be no doubt that youth has never lived under conditions of greater temptation than there are today and this applies most particularly to those who have not had a fair start in life or lack an adequate standard of education.

The Government should accept the unfortunate episode as a challenge to do more for youth.

Letters, Bruce Castle, Maroubra. Should the girl in such a case become pregnant, she is forced either to suffer further degradation in bearing the child of the assault or to commit a crime herself in order to terminate the pregnancy. In either case her chance of psychological or physical rehabilitation must be seriously impaired.

Society must face the question of legalised abortion, at least in such extreme cases.

WHAT SHOULD BE DONE ABOUT RAPE?

Whenever this question has been addressed in the past, one of the first suggestions has been that the criminals be given harsh punishment. Twenty years ago flogging was quite popular. Ten years ago, solitary confinement and harsh prison treatment were proposed.

Then again, second thoughts developed themes that said that parents and families were to blame. That the example set at home was damaging to young adults   Then some said the schools did not provide sex education, that youth clubs were not active enough, that there were too few social workers and psychologists, that gaoling young offenders simply confirmed them as being outside the law and opened them up to everything evil.

A few Letters suggest somewhat different approaches.

Letters, Vigilante, Merrylands. All girls should be quite clear in their minds that "entertainment" for groups of young men is likely to overtake them on our roads, at bus stops and around the suburbs unless they take the precaution of being adequately escorted.

Parents, too, should be aware that it is not necessarily the girl of low morals who is being sought; any girl, anywhere, is a likely victim of these gangs which move about in cars, panel vans or covered utilities on the lookout for unprotected girls. A girl has no hope of preventing herself from being forced into a vehicle by a number of strong young men, and once in the vehicle she has no hope of rescue or escape.

Another reader has a similar thought.

Letters, T Thomas, Roseville. The series of vicious and degenerate attacks, not only on girls but children, culminating in two fully grown males at Wagga being gaoled for rape of a 13-year-old child, cry aloud for special measures to meet this particular evil.

Many cases of rape arise out of girls being lured into cars and lorries. It should be an offence for men or boys – yes, boys, because a 15-year-old boy recently received a long sentence for rape – to attempt to entice a girl they do not know into a vehicle. Such legislation would advertise to all – girls, young men and parents – the incipiently criminal nature of luring girls into vehicles.

It is unsafe in many parts of Sydney for a young woman to walk in the street. The Judges are doing their duty; let the legislators do theirs.

Letters, Mother of Three, Northbridge. I note that one of the "Herald's" correspondents considers the recent life sentence for rape "savage," while another deplores the society that moulds these youths. All that is as it may be. The same society must present some strong deterrent against future crimes of such jungle ferocity.

While life imprisonment is a drain on the public purse, punishment by castration would surely be the most fitting penalty for these depraved young animals. If castration became the automatic punishment for sex attacks on women and little children, I am sure these ugliest of all crimes would disappear overnight.

I think our women's organisations are unrealistic and wishy-washy or they would surely campaign for harsh measures to combat a very real problem.

Letters, D Tregenza. Surely, Mother of Three's argument will bear some logical extension. Let us institute, for example, the cutting-off of hands as a punishment for crimes committed by those members, and the removal of the tongues of those found guilty of uttering slanderous words. Harsh measures – but surely effective deterrents!

The possibility, however remote, that an innocent person may be convicted of a crime and be obliged to forgo some appropriate part of his anatomy, which could not be restored to him on proof of his innocence, is a risk we will just have to take – after all, isn't our system of justice nearly infallible? Furthermore, seeing that the victim's life has been ruined, isn't it only fair that we should seek in exchange to ruin the criminal's?

I do not think so. Measures such as these not only would turn the clock back centuries in the matter of curing and preventing crime, but would be a fundamental negation of the Christian principles by which we as twentieth-century Westerners are supposed to live. For is it not basic to that creed (however imperfectly it is in fact applied in practice) that men, though sinful, are ultimately though sinful, are ultimately both worthy and capable of being made good? I cannot agree that cruel punishments are the answer to crime.

An effective stopgap measure for forestalling some crimes, and for achieving perhaps a number of other socially desirable purposes, may be to take some of the teenager's money away from him by, for example, a scheme of compulsory saving. But in the long run, we will have to take a good look at ourselves, too, and decide what our values and purposes for ourselves and our children are, and what they ought to be.

CHURCH OF ENGLAND: IS IT CATHOLIC ?

A few commentators have recently made the point that it was becoming acceptable to include the Church of England in with the Protestant Churches. This is particularly so in the Diocese of Sydney, more so than any other place in Australia.

Mr O'Keefe of Double Bay **acts as spokesman**. "The Anglican Communion in the Creeds declares her belief in the Holy Catholic and Apostolic Church. True the church was reformed of abuses that had kept in, but she retained Catholic practice in her orders, liturgy and theology. Nowhere in the Anglican prayer book is the word protestant to be found. It does appear once in the coronation service, but it was placed there for political rather than theological purposes.

"In 1951, the Primate of All England said that we have no doctrine of our own. We only possess the Catholic doctrine of the Catholic Church, and it is those creeds that we hold without addition or diminution."

These gentlemen represented above were much happier to be lumped in with the Catholics than with the Protestants, though I suspect there were many who felt differently.

RENTAL LAWS

There are 220,000 properties in NSW with rents pegged at 1939 levels. They were set at that level by the Federal Government, and thus similar laws still applied equally well to a few other States. The idea of fixing rents then was that this seemed a good way of controlling inflation during the war.

The consequence of this has been that tenants in those properties have had no rent increases for 25 years. Their families also have "a right of succession", which means that when they die, their existing rate of rental passes to their descendants. Clearly, this is a wonderful racket for the tenants.

For the landlords, however, it is a terrible deal. There has been an increase in the price of every other commodity, but their rental income has stayed put. They have responded by doing as few repairs as legally possible, and evicting tenants at the drop of a hat if they fall behind in their rents. In general, though, they were a bunch of losers with a legitimate grouch.

Politically, governments have been reluctant to change the situation. 220,000 voters is a big number, and the number of landlords is a lot less than that. Thus, no politician would like to be seen advocating an open market on rents.

The trouble now is that in NSW it appears that there will be some changes made. But given the political realities, the changes will be made to give more power to the tenants. In this case it means **making it harder for tenants to be evicted**. This of course will just perpetuate a bad system. While there are a few politicians around with more equitable suggestions, it seems at the moment that crude political survival will remain the order of the day. No wonder there is a shortage of good rental properties in the State.

Comment. In the 25 years since the start of WWII, **the Acts concerning rental of dwelling had been changed 50 times**. So when matters, like evictions and repairs to properties, came to court, the decisions were uncertain and chaotic.

In 1968, changes were made to various Acts so that agreements could be forced onto some tenants, and the right of inheritance was diminished. Also, the building of flats was somewhat encouraged. It was a bit clearer.

Given that over 50 percent of the population in 1964 were renting, any change to the status quo was important.

Letters, J Williams, Neutral Bay. From inquiries I have made and discussions in which I have taken part since reports have been published that the State Government is examining proposals to repeg 5A leases, I am convinced that if it interferes further with owners' rights this will spell political suicide for the NSW Labour Party.

Scores of thousands of owners, citizens and voters, will raise a public outcry which will have widespread repercussions and which could be the greatest single factor in bringing down the Government at the elections next year.

In other words, the action which some extreme Socialist-indoctrinated Labour members of Parliament are claiming would gain their party more voters will rebound like a boomerang and knock many of them into political oblivion.

The owners in NSW, big and small alike (and there are many who earn much less than many tenants), have just about reached breaking strain with the inferences, innuendoes, veiled threats and the like which are pumped out almost daily by some Labour members whose sole aim is to stay in power by parasitically hanging on to the apron strings of the "poor, oppressed tenant," who, by the way, has never had it better in any State in Australia.

Letters, Solicitor. Under the present Act all premises erected after 1954 are excluded from rent control, without registration under Section 5A. One hesitates to imagine that the Government would consider reintroducing controls of rents only in respect of buildings erected prior to 1954 and leave buildings erected later free from controls. Such registration would perpetuate the unfair discrimination against the owners of older properties.

NEWS AND TRIVIA

Letters, Corin Bass.   Can you tell me when will Australian sports men and women, their coaches, promoters and their adoring public learn that it is not necessary to deliver apologies and excuses for failures, and that sometimes the best man does win?

With each coming of the Olympic and Commonwealth Games, and minor events as well, we receive a barrage of boastful predictions of Australia's chances, with overwhelming importance given to the "smashing of records" by fractions of seconds – all quite out of proportion with what is surely the true aim and achievement in sportsmanship.

While persisting with this undue emphasis on sport, which regrettably begins and is fostered in schools, thus making the sportsman the hero and the intellectual the lesser man, Australia will continue to produce – with some obvious exceptions – a nation of cultural nonentities.

Letters, W Knight, Vaucluse. What does Mrs Corin Bass object to about sport – the sportsmen, the coaches, the commentator or the public? Or does she question the morality of having confidence in oneself?

Mrs Bass appears to lack nothing in self-confidence. With astonishing self-assurance she blasts every aspect of sport, including "the regrettable emphasis on sport fostered in schools."

Sport plays a very real part in the education of young people. I am associated with a swimming training squad which includes two school captains, several prefects and many quite brilliant students. Their devotion to sport does not appear to me to have affected adversely either their academic advancement or their sensitivity.

However, when a sportsman reaches world class he enters into another category. The subjection of the body by the rigorous and dedicated training necessary to reach this high standard enables the contender to attain a spiritual triumph. The same impulsion that enabled Edmund Hillary to conquer Mt Everest is the same that inspires young "sportsmen" to beat a time. The Murray Roses, Dawn Frasers, Don Bradmans, Herb Elliotts and Edmund Hillarys of all nations are not the dolts Mrs Bass would have us believe they are. They are using to the utmost the ability they have been given.

The crux of this subject of sport is not, as Mrs Bass says, that "sometimes the best man does win" but that the best man sometimes loses. It is in the ability of the loser to accept defeat graciously that the real value of sport is achieved.

I have had a long association with many sports and this spirit among sports men and women is highly developed.

Letters, Raymond Swanwick, Rose Bay. The news item reporting the death of Bob Whitelaw is correct in stating that Whitelaw beat Les Darcy on points over 20 rounds in 1913, but is not correct in stating that on that occasion Darcy "at 11st 4lb was a stone heavier" than Whitelaw.

With all due respect to the memory of Bob Whitelaw, the fact, as reported in the Newcastle "Herald" of November 4, 1913, was that Darcy weighed in at 10st 7lb and Whitelaw at 10st 6lb.

Darcy, who was only 18 years of age, had swollen hands, the result of a hard fight, nine days previously, in which he had beaten Billy McNabb in 20 rounds. Despite that, he hit Whitelaw so hard that he broke Whitelaw's rib.

Four months later, in a return bout on March 21, 1914, Darcy knocked Whitelaw out in the fifth round. I am writing a book on the life of Les Darcy. According to my researches, Darcy had 50 professional flights, and won 46 of them. He was never knocked out.

NOVEMBER NEWS ITEMS

Michelle Mason, of Sydney, became **the second woman in history to jump the six foot barrier**. She just cleared 6ft. The world record lies with a Romanian, with a jump of 6ft 3 inches.

Federal Parliamentarians just got a wage rise. Not surprisingly, there was **a flood of Letters to the SMH opposing it**. People were astonished, disgusted, envious, and bewildered. They talked about their meagre pensions, and said that, with inflation, they were going financially backward....

Many pointed out that **a big recent strike by GMH workers had achieved no increase**, and yet an increase had been granted here without any industrial action. One dissident writer said "most writers **are simply politician bashing**, and their Letters showed little grasp of anything that mattered." It was hard to disagree.

The Labour Party in Britain won the recent elections. They are moving immediately to **nationalise the steel industry**. In Australia, nationalisation and socialisation has been off the agenda for a decade. The question becomes will it come back to the fore? **Certainly, BHP and others will hope not.**

Tuesday Nov 4th. The big race was yesterday, and the winner was **the Democrat, Lyndon Johnston**. There was **also a horse race in Melbourne**, and there the winner was Polo Prince....

At the Melbourne races, **six women reported to the police that their dresses had been slashed by a man**

with a razor blade. A 52-year-old railways employee was arrested.

A man was whipped, another hit with a tomato stake, and a doctor injured by a stone that crashed into his mouth **when pro- and anti-fluoridation factions clashed at Grafton** (NSW) last night. The violence erupted at the showground where the Jacaranda Festival was being held.

Mr W Campbell today completed **19 years in Federal Parliament without missing a single day**.

Quote from the President of the Federation of Catholic Mothers' Club: we definitely think that **bikinis lower the resistance of young people to temptation**.

November 21st. **Dawn Fraser's horse won the Queensland Cup**. It was a present to her from her fiancé on their engagement.

A Federal Court jury in Miami, USA, has found that **cigarettes are "reasonably safe and wholesome for human consumption."** The civil court case was brought by the estate of the late Edward Green against the American Tobacco Company. It claimed that the **company's Lucky Strike cigarettes caused his death by cancer in 1957**.

If you want **a distilling kit for Christmas** so that you can distil whisky as you eat your turkey, then **you had better not**. Customs will get you and lock you up. From one who knows.

PROSTITUTION AS A SAFETY VALVE

One doctor was brave enough to propose an idea that has been round for a long time, but can scarcely be mentioned. I leave him to put the case for himself.

Letters, Doctor, Sydney. Having studied the relationship between prostitution and sex crimes in many countries of the world, I believe the recent increased incidence of rape and prowler attacks in Sydney is the natural result of the suppression of prostitution.

The Creator in His wisdom has given man a strong sex impulse, very necessary in the scheme of things, an urge which man-made laws cannot easily control. Many men are quite incapable of suppressing or sublimating this natural urge, with the horrifying results we have lately seen.

Prowlers are mainly perverts, a large proportion of whom, if they had had full opportunity for normal sex life at adolescence, would not have become perverts.

The police, acting on instructions from higher authorities, have chased prostitutes off the streets and in their zeal have even down cheaper brothels. However, prostitution still flourishes, but is now beyond the finances of the ordinary working man. While no one wants to see prostitutes roaming all over the city, they could be restricted to certain areas where they could be controlled, as is done in older cities throughout the world. This was the position in Sydney until recently.

In the past, prostitution was attributed to poverty and lack of employment. The fact that at the present day, with over-abundance of employment, women will want to take up this age-old profession shows that it has little to do with the economic situation. An important factor is that with present-day anti-venereal drugs the danger of infection has greatly diminished.

I ask the fathers of this community, if they think anything of the safety of their womenfolk, honestly to consider this question: If there had been a commonsense attitude to prostitution, how many women would have been spared the horrors of raping and pervert attacks?

Letters, A Robson, Chatswood. I cannot agree with the solution offered by "Doctor" to reduce the increased incidence of violence in the community.

What is needed in people is a real sense of the holiness of persons and of things. As the great scientist Professor C A Coulson said many times when he was here.

"This is God's world," and the persons and things in it are not here to be abused and wrecked, but to be respected and used for the good of all.

Religion and education can do their best but to not much avail when television, films, radio and literature combine to do their worst. When this sense is knocked into the heads of old and young alike (we are all in it), then the "vandalising" of human life, both male and female, will lessen.

Letters, A Davis. I, as the father of a young daughter, fully support the opinion of the Sydney doctor that prostitutes should be allowed to ply their trade in restricted areas. I feel sure that some of the mixed-up, over-sexed gangs of young louts would thus be able to appease the sexual appetite.

The incidence of rape has risen to an all-time record in our community and the police have done a splendid job in rounding up most of the culprits, but unless some other approach to this menace is adopted, I can see no end to these violent attacks on our womenfolk.

Unfortunately, some social workers, psychiatrists and ministers of religion, even though they profess to know so much about the age-old profession, can offer no sound solution for the abolition of the present-day gangs of louts who are always on the look-out for a "bird."

Letters, Interested, Campsie. I was pleased to see the related subjects of rape and prostitution dealt with by "Doctor" in the SMH last Tuesday.

When the police drive against prostitution began in earnest some months ago, it was freely predicted by people "in the business," and also by members of the Police Force itself, that the number of rape cases would rise. Were they right or wrong?

It would appear to be time that an authority other than the Vice Squad took a good hard look at the possible effects of present policy.

It cannot be argued that the controlled institution of prostitution would get rid of rape completely, but its abolition must surely affect this incidence of rape.

Letters, (Rev) B Archbold, Randwick. One fully appreciates the concern of A Davis for his young daughter. But whose daughter does he think should become the prostitute to be sacrificed in her interests? Mine? Or the "Doctor's"? or perhaps it would be more appropriate to have a wife and mother?

Surely we are not so insensitive that we forget that each prostitute is a person who should be regarded by a civilised community as much too sacred that she should be at the "convenience" of men! The answer to this serious sociological problem of "rape" is elsewhere.

Letters, Yet Another Doctor, Epping. The current discourse on the possible connection between suppression of prostitution and an outbreak of rape could be settled if it could be ascertained whether rapers in general have been unable to obtain sexual gratification with the consent of female partners on previous occasions. If they have been unsuccessful in the past, there may be something in what "Doctor" says. Otherwise they are sadists.

Comment. I expected a greater outcry against this, more than the letters above. I wonder why there were not more cries of condemnation?

SOME WARLIKE NEWS

I know that I promised you I would regale you with military matters only if some important news broke. About November 10th, some did. The Government announced that selective National Service would be introduced for 20-year-old males, starting in the middle of next year. **Importantly, it said it would change legislation so that these men could be sent overseas to serve in war zones.**

The selective system to be used would be that names would be **drawn from a hat until a quota of 4,200 men was reached**. In subsequent years, the number would be increased 6,900. Exemptions would be granted for apprentices and others yet to be decided, and certain essential industries would be protected against the drainage of manpower. Females would not be called up.

As the weeks went on, more details were announced. All persons balloted would serve for two years, and then for three years part-time with the CMF. University students would be exempt. If a person was not selected in a first ballot, they would not be included in next year's ballot. It might be that bigger intakes would become necessary in the years ahead.

As might be expected, there were some objections. There was a suggestion that calling up 18-year-olds would cause less disruption than 20-year-olds. Currently, over 60 per cent of the volunteers for the CMF were rejected because of the low educational standard. The standard required would have to be dropped. Married men would surely be excused. What about engaged men?

Other advice proffered included that new graduates in law and medicine and dentistry needed their first year of on-the-job training to finish their degrees. Surely they should be exempt. Why make non-naturalised aliens not eligible for call-up?. They live here and work here. Surely they should be prepared to solder here. The number selected is not enough. It should be doubled.

One gentleman put some arguments that you might or might not agree with.

Letters, H Dowsett. One reads with interest and sympathy the welter of letters in your columns and on Thursday morning there came to me still one more aspect of the vexed question. It was announced that an American fighter plane in South Vietnam had been shot down by Reds and that an intensive ground search was being made for the American pilot.

Now, in view of the ANZUS Treaty and the fact that America's armed forces are in part maintained by conscription, I submit the time has arrived when we should ask ourselves the following questions:

(a) If conscription is apparently a good thing in keeping America strong; why do some Australians believe conscription for Australians, with liability for overseas service, as in America, not so good?

(b) Do we in Australia, in New Zealand, and in Britain, tend to allow America to do just a little too much for the defence of the free world while we, all three, tend to be concerned just a little too much with social services, the pursuit of pleasure, gambling, etc.?

(c) Would it be some consolation for the American parents of the abovementioned lone American airman if they could receive the assurance that for the future we are determined to do just a little more for the defence of the free world --- even though it means conscription in our land?

One final point. The Leader of the Labour Party, Arthur Calwell, fell back on an old Party policy and said that our conscripts should not be sent to fight overseas. He intends to make this the major issue in the upcoming Senate elections.

Which raises the question of the minimum voting age. Currently, it is 21 years. That means that the young men who will be conscripted, perhaps to fight overseas, will not have a vote in those same Senate elections.

Comment. I intend to maintain my reluctance to give you more military news unless it is vital. Here's hoping.

DRINKING AND THE YOUNG

A Headmaster of a Sydney GPS Boys' High School gave the opinion that alcohol should be banned at the end-of-year parties for final-year students. That is, that boys, or young men, of 17 and 18 years of age, should not be allowed to drink alcohol at these functions. He raised it in connection with driving, and was not motivated by any wowser reaction to drinking, but by concern for the welfare of the young men.

A young man, a Mr Evans of Clifton Gardens, took issue with this opinion. He thinks that it is foolish to expect that boys of that age should be restricted to drinking orange juice. If that is the case, he asks, at what age will they be allowed? In another month? In six months? In two years? What is the right age? Is one lessening the danger of drinking and driving by postponing the starting age?

He goes on to say that the answer is to introduce children to drinking over a period of years. For example, **by allowing wine at the dinner table when they first start school**.

He says that it is futile to simply ban boys from doing anything that they will do in any case. It is more sensible to introduce some form of compromise rather than an outright prohibition.

This was a growing social problem. There was at the time not much recognition that drinking played such an important role in causing crashes. This was **before the universal imposition of breath testing**, a period where almost everyone thought that he might drive **even better** with a few beers inside. It was before we all became conscious of the .15 or .12 alcohol content restriction, then the .07, then the current .05 rule. **Everyone** affected by alcohol was close to immortal. Youth, always immortal, was immortal with brass knobs on.

So, there were words of moderation forthcoming from a few parents.

Letters, Lilian Craft, Cammeray. Gradual introduction of children to liquor is, however, not the solution. Indeed, the contrary. In France, where the practice is widespread, alcoholism has become a social problem of alarming proportions with a frightening number of child alcoholics.

The responsibility of parents is inescapable. They can introduce their children to liquor (described by a medical authority as the No. 1 drug of addiction) or show by their own mode of living that drinking is neither essential not inevitable. Also, that there can be gay and happy parties without it.

Conceding to Mr Evans his point regarding boys, that they will at some stage drink and smoke, if they have a desire to do so, it must also be conceded that they have the right to refrain from those habits if they desire to do so.

The great difference is that it requires far more will-power, conviction and skill to serenely refrain in face of constant and massive pressures to indulge. Many parents add their weight to this pressure when they could with advantage show their children how to offer and accept hospitality with courtesy and cheerfulness, but without the aid of alcohol.

Letters, Mrs E Webb, Wahroonga. The cool assumption expressed by Paul Evans who left school two years ago, that all youngsters are going to be drinkers and should therefore be educated at an early age to "take" it, expresses a point of view which is, unfortunately, becoming more and more widespread.

Why must the drinking of alcohol at parties be considered the right thing to do? There must be many young people who would prefer their personalities to be truly expressed and not falsified and distorted by artificial means. Are we giving these youngsters a fair go, or are they becoming pressurised into doing what everyone else expects them to do?

There will always be drinkers, in any country, in any community, in most parties, and their antics are often good for a laugh, but it doesn't necessarily follow that all members must drink alcohol too. What is needed is a more moderate, more tolerant attitude to non-drinkers. Let it be a matter of commendation if our children stand out against the mob.

HANDRAIL AT AYERS ROCK

Letters, Guy Moore. I learn from news over the radio that the Commonwealth Government Department in charge of Ayers Rock has placed a handrail on the rock to enable visitors to climb it.

When it was announced some while back that a chair lift was to be placed on the rock there was considerable objection on the part of both the public and conservation bodies, so much so that this was abandoned. Those people concerned with the preservation of this glorious monolith were heartened by this action of the Government, believing, quite mistakenly, that no further attempt at defacement would be undertaken. However, defacement has been achieved, quietly, without notice to either the public or to those bodies concerned with its preservation in its natural state.

The stigma for this action must rest solidly on the shoulders (would that it were on their heads) of the department concerned no matter who the instigators were or are.

That it has been defaced to make a tourists' plaything warrants the most severe condemnation. It is to be hoped that sufficient public anger at this action will be generated to have this excrescence removed before the rock becomes a signboard for its thousands of visitors who in most places leave their un-honoured names behind them.

Letters, Rock-Lover. Guy Moore speaks with great authority of the "defacement" of our "glorious monolith," Ayers Rock. As it is only a matter of weeks since I returned from Ayers Rock and was fortunate enough to climb it with the use of the railing which has caused Mr Moore so much anguish, I feel qualified to condemn his words.

The railings consist of two short sections of small metal rods joined by chain and have been placed only on two very dangerous stretches of the rock. From the ground they are barely visible and from the air it is impossible to see them, but to the tourist, who, for Mr Moore's benefit, pays for the railing, they are invaluable.

To remove them because a group of citizens who have never seen them find them objectionable would be criminal. To realise that this is so, one has only to speak to the rangers and guides who on two occasions in the past have had to recover the bodies of those who have fallen.

NEWS AND TRIVIA

Letters, E Legg. Never in the history of Sydney have so many women been seen wearing laddered stockings as at present.

The reason must be that it is becoming well nigh impossible to buy a pair of stockings which will give reasonable wear owing to the insistence of the manufacturers that we all prefer seamless 12 or 15 denier stockings to the fully fashioned 30 denier of the past which would stand up to some wear and tear without laddering.

And we haven't all got the good-looking legs to carry off sheer either. Many of us prefer something a little more substantial, especially when it comes to fighting our way on and off public transport in the peak hours.

Letters, Tom Nelson, Waterside Workers' Federation of Aust., Sydney. On Monday, a frightful tragedy was averted when a powerful time-bomb was discovered in a city premises. People within the building, in nearby workplaces and residences, and passers-by in the street were faced with death or grave injury had the bomb not been detected in time.

It is alarming that the morning Press of this city was not concerned enough to express any criticism of such a treacherous criminal action. Was this because the bomb was directed against the working-class centre of the Communist Party?

Any organisation is vulnerable if this sort of action, unprecedented in Australia's history, is unchallenged by Press and public condemnation.

Letters, Ken Williams, Drag-ens Rod and Kustom Club, Croydon Park. "Drag racing on public streets is hoodlum driving and must be stopped." This statement, made by Superintendent J McCloskey, appeared in the article "War On Hoodlum Drivers" in the "Sun-Herald" on November 15.

How will it be stopped? While young people are interested in having their cars a little better than the next guy, they will drag. The only way to stop drag racing on the streets is to give these young people a suitable enclosed area where legal drags may be held under strict supervision.

In America, drag racing started with hot-rods (early model cars, modified with late model engines and reworked suspension) competing in pairs over a quarter of a mile for the fastest acceleration time, but today most of the drag-racing program consists of late model, hotted-up cars as seen on our roads today.

This type of racing caters for the average motorist with a safe car, but it is not yet available in New South Wales. The nearest drag strip where drag-racing enthusiasts can race their hot-rods and other hot cars is Riverside Dragway at Fishermen's Bend in Melbourne. Dragging has proved both successful and popular at Riverside under the strict supervision of the Victorian Police and the Victorian Hot Rod Association.

The hot-rodders' main complaint is the confusion between true hot-rods and the normal run of hot sedans and noisy jalopies. Every time a complaint reaches the newspapers concerning some rusted-out heap with a lowered suspension and a noisy muffler they are referred to as hot-rods. These are not hot-rods.

Most hot-rods in the Sydney area belong to well-organised clubs with their first emphasis on safety. These clubs are striving for a good name and the promotion of organised drag racing, the safest competitive motor sport in the world. Hoodlum driving and hooliganism will not be tolerated in these clubs.

As hot-rodders we would request that the name hot-rod should not be used where it does not apply.

DECEMBER NEWS ITEMS

December 1st. **It is Winston Churchill's 90th birthday today.** He received appropriate messages from the Queen, President Johnson, and 50 other heads of State.

The new religious instruction syllabus will be introduced early next year. It will retain the controversial coverage of religions other than Christianity. The Anglican Archbishop of Sydney said that he was **"delighted and completely satisfied"** by it.

Pope Paul IV was mobbed when he arrived at Bombay airport. He is **the first Pope to visit Asia** and the 4,000 mile journey from Rome was the longest ever taken by any Pope.

A bale of **wool so fine that it resembled silk** was sold for **over 7 Pounds per pound.** This was triple the previous record price. Mr Trevor Picker said that the wool was taken from 120 specially selected sheep.

December 5th . **The Government, led by Menzies, did well in the half-Senate elections** and retained its hold there of 31-29.

December 6th. **A High Court judgement today** which, if applied, would mean an average increase of **100 per cent in the rent for 100,000 controlled properties**, was handed down today. The Court said that the rent set should **take into consideration the value of the property**, which had increase by at least 100 per cent since 1939....

Monday, December 9th. The NSW Government, by special decree, negated **the High Court judgement**

until appeals could be made to the Privy Council in London. In the meantime, rents for controlled properties **would still be frozen at 1939 rates.**

December 9th. **TAB betting started today at TAB offices,** five in Sydney and one in Newcastle. A network of branches will be established across the State, **owned and operated by individual businessmen.** Corporate bodies like racing clubs, companies, and churches would not be allowed to run them.

Lightning struck three airliners in freak weather in Victoria. In one, 80 passengers were aboard a Comet as it flew over the You Yang Ranges. The lightening ripped a 4-foot hole in the radar dome in the nose of the aircraft.

A reminder that strikes have not gone away. The Government has at last ordered the strikers at Mount Isa back to work, after 15 weeks. The smelter produces two-thirds of Australia's copper requirements.

Actor Percy Kilbride, who found fame in the Ma and Pa Kettle TV series, died on 12th December, aged 76.

The NSW Milk Board is prepared to heavily **subsidise the refrigeration of free milk in the schoolyards.** It is hoped that this will encourage children to drink it.

Of course. A strike by the Transport Workers Union will **disrupt most of Sydney's Christmas deliveries today.** 12,000 men will be involved, and will stop deliveries of most items, including chickens, hams and turkeys. The strike is for one day, but militants are trying to extend it to a general strike.

TIDYING UP A FEW THINGS

The Voyager incident. The naval community was not happy with the first Voyager Royal Commission. It was most unhappy about the treatment handed out to Commander Robinson. At the same time, morale in the Navy fell to low levels. Over 1965, matters festered, including the claim that the commander of the Voyager was not fit to serve at the time, until a second Royal Commission was begun in 1967.

To close this matter out, the Melbourne was involved in a second collision with a USS, Frank E Evans. 74 US Naval personnel died, and once again the commander of the Melbourne was scapegoated. But that is another story.

War games. The belligerency continued on, and so too did the arms build up and the troop flows. No one seemed to be interested in promoting common sense, and it looked like another trial of strength between Capitalism and Communism was coming. Why not? After all, wars are good for business, and it is good that they can now be waged on other people's territory. It had worked in Korea. Why not another variation, say in Vietnam this time?

In fact, as many of you will recall, the gradual build up in hostilities continued and accelerated, with our involvement increasing to a battalion in 1965, and full scale fighting in 1966. The Vietnam War was on.

Late shopping hours. Thirty-odd shopkeepers had warrants issued for their arrests so far, though there appears a reluctance to enforce them. Also, five hairdressers had similar warrants outstanding. Mr Renshaw and his government were making confusing noises about allowing some traders under certain conditions to open up late, but there was no sign of a consistent policy as yet.

Dawn Fraser. This winner of four gold medals over three meetings was arrested in Tokyo for stealing an Olympic flag from the Emperor's Palace. She was not charged. After a bit of hush-hush, the Olympic Committee suspended her for 10 years. They reduced this to four, but not quite in time for her to train properly for the 1968 Olympics.

The Labour Party. There are a number of Labour Party executives and branches calling for the resignation of Arthur Calwell as leader of the Federal Labour Party. Voices in Queensland are loudest. It will doubtless come to nothing. The main thing to be learned from such confusion is that the Labour Party will have to face 1965 in a divided state.

SOME ADVANCED IDEAS FOR OZ

At the end of every book, I indulge myself, and let myself ramble for a few pages. Most often, I fulminate against the foolishness of war. I will probably do that again next year after the Vietnam war gets into swing. This year, however, I will dwell on the time I spent a few months ago with an old-timer from Albury. Mr Kent showed me a letter he had written in 1964, and it was published in a Melbourne newspaper. I enclose it here, and will comment on it later.

"As we get close to Christmas, I want to give Australia a gift. I am giving you below a glimpse of my wisdom, and if you heed it, every Australian will be immeasurably better off.

"I will limit myself to three projects because I know that you collectively have a short span that you can concentrate in. I know too that half of you have no idea of policy formation, and always evaluate proposals with a mixture of pre-conceived results, and from a point of what's in it for me. To these people I suggest that you don't read this letter. Go chase a greyhound dog.

"Three proposals for those who can think. **First,** Australia needs to harness its water supply. I do not care where we take it from, or where we pump it to. Just accept that we need it, and work out the details. Can we afford it? Of course we can. Just spend the money, and we can inflate our way out of our debt like other big nations do. Of course we can afford it.

"**Second.** The world needs food. Stop playing round at the edges. Decide that we as a nation are food producers, and shut up and grow it. On a huge scale. Can we sell it? Of course we can. Just say we have got the produce and go out and sell it. Someone will sell the food. It should be us.

"**Third.** We need to develop our fishing industry. By that I don't mean we should go out with nets and drag the fish in. We need to grow our own, from fishlings, and crablings and lobsterlings, and so on. We've got all this coastline, we can use some bit of it, somewhere, to raise and grow and sell any fish product we like. If we can't grow lobsters in South Australia, we can grow them in Western Australia, somewhere.

"What this government needs to do is pick some enterprises, and say that we will start such-and-such an industry. Then provide the money for it, and let private initiative gradually take over. If we can't finance it straight away, borrow it. Everyone else borrows all the time. Let the government borrow to the hilt, and get some industries moving."

Comment. Mr Kent tells me that at the time, in 1964, he got mixed responses. The idea that the nation should pump its water from wet spots to dry spots, he says, got almost universal approval. The logic of it is obvious "to blind Freddie", and everyone wonders why we haven't done it.

As for agriculture, most people said we had done that already. They had horizons bounded by wheat and wool, and it seemed that that was all they thought we should grow,

The "fish-in ponds" idea got no support at all. Could not be done, they all said. Tides and floods and predators and diseases would destroy anyone who tried.

There was no support for the government to borrow big to start new projects. It was not the role of governments to meddle in new businesses. Also, they simply are no good at doing so.

Second comment. I found all of this interesting. In Australia, at the time, the main game was to keep things on an even keel, and if we had any new businesses, or new ideas, they should all come from overseas. New capital should come from there as well. The idea that the Government should take the bull by the horns, and try some new ventures, was just not within the thinking of Joe Blow. As Australian author Donald Horne said at the time, in 1964, we were a lucky country. I agree with him, and I add that we hoped we could keep very still and stay that way. Given the happenings in Asia above, that might not be a bad idea.

THE SNOWY TUNNEL

After thanking you for your indulgence during my ramblings, I should acknowledge the end of a giant engineering feat in the Snowy Mountains of NSW. This was a project that was daringly conceived and brilliantly executed.

News item. The opening of the last link of the 32-mile tunnel complex in the Snowy scheme proved to be a hair-raising and foot-soaking experience for the official party.

Mr Fairbairn opened the nine-mile tunnel from the Geehi Reservoir to the Murray One power station on the headwaters of the Murray River. It is the last stage of an unbroken waterway of 32 miles from Lake Eucumbene, by way of Island Bend.

To get to the remaining tunnel wall, the official party rode on trams to a point 3,000ft below the peaks of the Australian Alps, and almost at the power station end. They then splashed 1,000 yards through water up to a foot deep to the tunnel face.

There, Mr Fairbairn exploded 800lb of gelignite to break through the last few feet of the tunnel. The blast was a huge success. It blew out the partition, and blew off the fibreglass safety helmet of every guest. The helmets landed in the water. There was a scramble as many of the guests retrieved their helmets hastily and jammed them back on their heads, overlooking that they were full of water.

It was a damp but jovial party which emerged from the tunnel soon afterwards. Some sat down, took off their shoes and socks and wrung them out, but several hours later most of the party were squelching about with their shoes full of water.

Mr Fairbairn said the 32 miles of tunnelling was completed at a cost of £1million a mile.

CHRISTMAS IS HERE

It's here again. This year the newspapers are carrying more stories on women fainting in the crush in city stores. This might be a carry-over from the Beatles. The papers are also full of complaints about the playing of carols that have no connection with Christ, and the fact that Christmas itself falls into the same secular trap. There are lots of Letter writers who see the value of a few hours in church on Christmas Day, and the dangers of the idolatory of sport over the holidays. Indeed, one writer promised tennis players that they would end up in Hell if they took up their racquets on that day.

Retail trade was doing well, city crowds were stifling, and public transport was impossible. Beer drinkers could not get much bottled beer. Children were sitting on Santa's knee, and the ones that did not scream seemed to enjoy it. In all, the build-up to the big event was normal, the day itself was as stressful as you would expect, and for me, the box of men's handkerchiefs was much better than the ladies' box I got last year.

One gentleman wanted to emphasise some traps that people fell into.

Letters, Colin Ritchie. Young people should be free from **unfair social pressure to start drinking**. There is a growing number of people for whom alcohol is a problem and they can be helped by removing the pressure at parties.

The mounting toll of the road. Drinking is one factor and any amount is excessive for the driver, particularly in Christmas traffic conditions. Management has a responsibility to the family, particularly young folk, to see that staff members arrive home safely.

Restrict the sometimes **excessive expenditure on personal indulgence** by supporting some of the **worthy charitable and church causes** which remind us that Christmas is not self-indulgence but self-limitation and sacrifice for others.

Alcohol does not of itself ensure a happy or successful party. It **is often associated with boredom and sameness, even drabness**.

This is not an appeal for dullness, but for virile committees which will not take the easy way of placing a big order for strong drink, but which will do some constructive planning to make our business and social parties at Christmas bright occasions which **will not degenerate into a hangover of spinning heads and behaviour to be regretted the next morning.**

WOMEN'S CHRISTMAS PARTIES

To add my own little bit to the Christmas festivities, I enclose the Letters below. It is good to see that in this time of goodwill to all, men and women can bury the hatchet and find common ground for discussion.

Letters, Charles Murray. May we pause in our endless entanglement with the international situation, the economic situation and the political situation to reflect a moment on something which closely affects our domestic happiness, our marital security and our Australian way of life?

I refer to the Christmas antics of what John Knox called The Monstrous Regiment Of Women.

Go into the city any evening at this time of the year and one is awed, surprised and dismayed at the spectacle of the numerous groups of women, made up like film stars, dressed like fashion models and giggling like schoolgirls, who parade our streets in a macabre March Of The Matriarchs. These are the suburban tennis clubs, the women's guilds, the chapters, the "fizzy" groups, out for their annual "do."

They have dinner at the most expensive restaurants, followed by the best seats at a leading theatre with a little window-shopping in between. All of this with nary a man to chaperon, protect or amuse them. The men, poor devils, are at home minding the children, working on the night-shift or slaving over a hot poker-machine.

Let any husband mention a night at the theatre around this time and he will invariably be told, "Oh no, not that one. The girls might be going there." This deprivation of free choice, this female-inspired sex-segregation, this unbalanced, unnatural and uncivilised tribal custom is fast **reaching the proportions of a major social crime.**

Letters, Dolly. What is wrong with women in the over-40 group dressing up and meeting together to have dinner and a theatre party and a good laugh? Don't men ever have a night out at the club or the pub?

Lots of these women are single or widows, not all have a devoted husband at home. And just where are the men to escort the ladies; where are they found? It is most unkind to presume that all these women without escorts like it that way.

Most bachelors or widowers in the middle age group prefer to console their lonely existence with expensive female models of a very youthful vintage. A capable woman who keeps a tidy home and garden and cooks well and has a sense of humour and loves dinner in town and a theatre just doesn't get invited out by the "poor lonely mate" unless she keeps advertising herself in hotels, holiday resorts and cruises. And if she is a working woman she has only three weeks a year to get her man.

Letters, Susan Campbell, Merrylands. They want us women to be mature and independent, and to help us to achieve this they give us the most difficult tasks requiring an enormous amount of patience and fortitude (i.e. bringing up children; they allow us to stand shoulder to shoulder with them in public transport; some have even suggested conscription).

And then when we go off on our own they bleat like most lambs. The poor darlings have got to learn that's the way the cookie crumbles. A little maturity and independence is a dangerous thing.

Letters, Win Robbins. As a "Matriarch" of some 11 years' standing, I might state that your correspondence reflects the attitude of many of his sex although few have the courage to make light of these women's outings. I would like the opposite sex to be aware of the organisation and grim determination that eventually make this outing such a memorable occasion.

From the first week in January we are obliged – somehow or other – to deduct from our often miserable housekeeping allowance the sum of two shillings a week. A treasurer is appointed and proper accounts are kept. At the end of the year, after great deliberation, we choose the best eating-house and entertainment our savings will provide. Then we have the major task of "running up" some inexpensive dress or reverting once again to the "good black".

With all this arranged we set the date, which we finally impart to the "old man" knowing that on this night he is to be keeper of his kids. To his horror he remembers he, too, has a function on this same night. But, undaunted, we read the riot act and for the sake of a peaceful Yule-tide we win out.

So, it is with pride that I watch my fellow "matriarchs" sipping the "giggly", passing around the lifesavers, and generally having a thoroughly well-earned good time.

Letters, Dolly-less, Canberra. Where, oh where, are these capable women (unattached) who keep a tidy home, etc, and have all the attributes that "Dolly" claims?

I am a widower of 42, well educated, widely travelled, have my own home, car and other assets, and am in a high-salaried executive position. Search as I may I have been unable to find these paragons of the female sex. Homely widows years older than myself, yes, "expensive females of youthful vintage" – no; they want the fast-driving, slow-thinking youths of similar age to themselves. They have told me so.

The woman of 40 or so who enjoys the theatre, a night out, and can talk about anything apart from babies, housework and recipes does not exist in the unattached state. Certainly not in Sydney or Canberra; certainly not where I have looked.

Comment. The question is just where did those men and women bury the hatchet? In each other?

THE END OF A GOOD YEAR

Donald Horne's famous book, *The Lucky Country*, painted a picture of a country that was having good fortune, but scarcely deserved it. Between him and the Arnolds' Letter in June, we were found to be insular, not hard-working, self-interested, and more-or-less empty-headed. Horne added that our leaders were second-rate.

I am quite at ease with all of this. I agree with Slim Williams' reply in June that we have no need to get anxious and morbid until there is some good reason. I agree with those Beatle-lovers who say that we could pull our sox up, as did this entire nation in WWII, if the chips were again down.   I agree with the old-timer, Mr Kent, in December, who argued for more active government participation in the long-term planning and active running of the country.

I also agree with Horne that our elected representatives are second-rate. Some of them are good, but many, many more are not. **At the national level**, the arguments over who are the goodies and who are the baddies go on and on. **At the State level**, corruption and preference are eternal. **The local Councils** are packed with vested interests, and intellectual dwarfs. It is a lacklustre scene. One compensation is that there is no suggestion that any jurisdiction, anywhere in the world, is any different.

Having said that, it still seems to me that we remained lucky in 1964. You all know how to count your blessings, and I will just mention jobs, housing, peace, prosperity, freedom, and plenty. We had them this year in abundance. If we were irritated by strikes, and by the silly decisions of politicians looking after their own Parties and interests, then compared to all our blessings, those are small beer.

You will have seen that this happy state will not last. Sadly, day by day over the last few months, the dreaded spectre of a major war has edged closer to us. The forces of Capitalism and Communism are ready to show off their might again, as in Korea, and will keep pushing each other in Vietnam till they get into another scrap that each of them comes to regret. Our problem is that our own young men will get caught up in this, and will be sent off to be killed and mutilated, all to no avail.

If you can put this out of your mind, I think you were lucky indeed to be born in 1964. I can't think of a better time, or a better place, to be born, and I commend you for your wise choice.

COMMENTS FROM READERS

Tom Lynch, Spears Point…..Some history writers make the mistake of trying to boost their authority by including graphs and charts all over the place. You on the other hand get a much better effect by saying things like "he made a pile". Or "every one worked hours longer that they should have, and felt like death warmed up at the end of the shift." I have seen other writers waste two pages of statistics painting the same picture as you did in a few words….

Barry Marr, Adelaide….you know that I am being facetious when I say that I wish the war had gone on for years longer so that you would have written more books about it…

Edna College, Auburn…. A few times I stopped and sobbed as you brought memories of the postman delivering letters, and the dread that ordinary people felt as he neared. How you captured those feelings yet kept your coverage from becoming maudlin or bogged down is a wonder to me….

Betty Kelly. Every time you seem to be getting serious you throw in a phrase or memory that lightens up the mood. In particular, in the war when you were describing the terrible carnage of Russian troops, you ended with a ten line description of how aggrieved you felt and ended it with "apart from that, things are pretty good here". For me, it turned the unbearable into the bearable, and I went from feeling morbid and angry back to a normal human being….

MORE INFORMATION ON THESE BOOKS

Over the past 16 years the author, Ron Williams, has written this series of books that present a social history of Australia in the post-war period. They cover the period for 1939 to 1973, with one book for each year. Thus there are 35 books.

To capture the material for each book, the author, Ron Williams, worked his way through the Sydney Morning Herald and The Age/Argus day-by-day, and picked out the best stories, ideas and trivia. He then wrote them up into 184 pages of a year-book.

He writes in a direct conversational style, he has avoided statistics and charts, and has produced easily-read material that is entertaining, and instructive, and charming.

They are invaluable as gifts for birthdays, Christmas, and anniversaries, and for the oldies who are hard to buy for.

AVAILABLE FROM ALL GOOD BOOK STORES

AND NEWSAGENTS

In 1956, the first big issue was the Suez crisis, which put our own Bob Menzies on the world stage, but he got no applause. TV was turned on in time for the Melbourne Olympics, Hungary was invaded and the Iron Curtain got a lot thicker. There was much concern about cruelty to sharks, and the horrors of country pubs persisted.

In 1958, the Christian brothers bought a pub

and raffled it; some clergy thought that Christ would not be pleased. Circuses were losing animals at a great rate. Officials were in hot water because the Queen Mother wasn't given a sun shade. Chrissi and birthday books for Mum and Dad and Aunt and Uncle and cousins and family and friends and work and everyone else. School milk was hot news, bread home deliveries were under fire. The RSPCA was killing dogs in a gas chamber. A tribe pointed the bone at Albert Namatjira; he died soon after.

DON'T FORGET A GOOD READ FOR YOURSELF